ON THE SIGNIFICANCE OF RELIGION FOR THE SDGs

This timely volume addresses the rising interest in the role of religion in global issues worldwide. The ambitious Agenda 2030 and the 17 Sustainable Development Goals (SDGs) serve as the framework for this exploration, discussing questions such as:

- What role does religion play in poverty and poverty alleviation?
- How does religion inspire people in combatting gender inequality?
- What is religion's role in fueling conflict and which resources can religion offer for peace and reconciliation?

Based on the conviction that not one single faith tradition or discipline can adequately address the complexity of current global issues, this book brings in the perspectives of different faith traditions and different disciplines.

Combining cutting-edge research with case studies and concrete implications for academics, policymakers, and practitioners, this concise and easily accessible volume helps to build bridges between these different actors and their engagement. It serves as the introductory volume to the series, *Religion Matters: On the Significance of Religion in Global Issues*.

Christine Schliesser is a Senior Lecturer at Zurich University. She is the Director of Studies at the Center for Faith & Society at Fribourg University and a Research Fellow in Studies in Historical Trauma and Transformation at Stellenbosch University.

Religion Matters: On the Significance of Religion in Global Issues

Edited by:
Christine Schliesser, *Zurich University, Switzerland*
S. Ayse Kadayifci-Orellana, *Georgetown University, USA*
Pauline Kollontai, *York St. John University, UK*

Policymakers, academics, and practitioners worldwide are increasingly paying attention to the role of religion in global issues. This development is clearly noticeable in conflict resolution, development or climate change, to name just a few pressing issues of global relevance. Up to now, no book series has yet attempted to analyze the role of religion in current global issues in a coherent and systematic way that pertains to academics, policy makers, and practitioners alike. The Sustainable Development Goals (SDGs) serve as a dynamic frame of reference. "Religion Matters" provides cutting edge scholarship in a concise format and accessible language, thereby addressing academics, practitioners, and policy makers.

On the Significance of Religion in Conflict and Conflict Resolution
Christine Schliesser, S. Ayse Kadayifci-Orellana, and Pauline Kollontai

On the Significance of Religion for Global Diplomacy
Philip McDonagh, Kishan Manocha, John Neary, and Lucia Vázquez Mendoza

On the Significance of Religion in Violence Against Women and Girls
Elisabet le Roux and Sandra Iman Pertek

On the Significance of Religion in Deliberative Democracy
Kudakwashe Chitsike, Ruby Quanston Davis, and Elizabeth Gish

On the Significance of Religion for the SDGs: An Introduction
Christine Schliesser

On the Significance of Religion for Human Rights
Pauline Kollontai and Friedrich Lohmann

For more information about this series, please visit: https://www.routledge.com/religion/series/RELMAT

"*Religion Matters* makes a forceful case that a deeply embedded consideration of religious approaches to development thinking and action needs to be a central part of the international development landscape. Primarily through the lens of the United Nations Sustainable Development Goals (SDGs), the analysis focuses on both strengths and weaknesses that the myriad of religious institutions and communities bring to specific challenges. It offers well thought-out-frameworks to help policy makers as they navigate the complex religious worlds that include both powerful core ideas and fodder for ample controversy and, more hopefully, dialogue."

Katherine Marshall, *Senior Fellow, Berkley Center for Religion, Peace, and World Affairs, Georgetown University, USA; Executive Director, World Faiths Development Dialogue*

"This book highlights the important role that religion can play in achieving the SDGs as well as some of the pitfalls. It combines social science and theological approaches with 'spotlights' on particular topics from practitioners in the field to underscore the fact that religion matters for development and needs to be taken seriously. In contrast to many other texts in this field, the contributors are all 'insider voices' and 'imminent critics' of the faith traditions they write about. This volume, therefore, brings a fresh approach for academics, policymakers, and practitioners interested in the relationships between religion and the SDGs."

Emma Tomalin, *Professor of Religion and Public Life, University of Leeds, UK*

"This book seeks to build bridges across the secular-religious divide and between the different spheres of engagement in development, including academics, policymakers, and practitioners. The authors develop this aim in two parts: Part 1: The rise of religion and development and Part 2: Religion and the sustainable development goals. The book engages these two topics in 12 chapters from many different religious perspectives making it a wonderful example of interreligious dialogue and putting the spotlight on many different contentious and contested issues around the globe. This kind of collaborative form of research on religion and development gives expression to an African (isiXhosa) saying: 'The bird builds its nest by using other birds'."

Ian Nell, *Professor of Practical Theology, Stellenbosch University, South Africa*

"The issue of the relationship between religion and the SDGs is a crucial topic, not least because the influence of the former may be crucial in achieving the latter. In this volume, Christine Schliesser analyses the role of religion in the SDGs. The book is a welcome addition to the growing literature on the role of religion in development and should be of particular interest to students and the general reader."

Jeffrey Haynes, *Emeritus Professor of Politics, London Metropolitan University, UK*

"Religion is embedded in every expression of human culture around the globe and, in spite of increasing secularism, religion continues to be a major influence for the vast majority of people in the world today. So, if we are to achieve the ambition of the Agenda 2030 with the 17 SDGs, it's essential to consider religion in every aspect of development. This book provides an excellent introduction for policymakers and practitioners, it builds bridges across the secular-religious divide and encourages faith communities to work together to address complex issues."

Tony Macaulay, *Northern Ireland Author, Leadership Consultant, Peace Builder, and Broadcaster*

"This book comprises of recent advancements in development theory and practice. It embraces vital discussions on gender equality, poverty, inequality, peace, and justice, all of which are fundamental in understanding the significance of religion in development. These discourses take place in a network of global dialogue, involving voices from various faith traditions."

Auli Vähäkangas, *Professor in Practical Theology, University of Helsinki, Finland*

ON THE SIGNIFICANCE OF RELIGION FOR THE SDGs

An Introduction

Christine Schliesser

LONDON AND NEW YORK

Designed cover image: Cover by Schwarzfalter GmbH www.schwarzfalter.ch

First published 2023
by Routledge
4 Park Square, Milton Park, Abingdon, Oxon OX14 4RN

and by Routledge
605 Third Avenue, New York, NY 10158

Routledge is an imprint of the Taylor & Francis Group, an informa business

© 2023 Christine Schliesser

The right of Christine Schliesser to be identified as author of this work has been asserted in accordance with sections 77 and 78 of the Copyright, Designs and Patents Act 1988.

The Open Access version of this book, available at www.taylorfrancis.com, has been made available under a Creative Commons Attribution-Non Commercial-No Derivatives 4.0 license.

Published with the support of the Swiss National Science Foundation (SNSF)

Trademark notice: Product or corporate names may be trademarks or registered trademarks, and are used only for identification and explanation without intent to infringe.

British Library Cataloguing-in-Publication Data
A catalogue record for this book is available from the British Library

ISBN: 978-1-032-36493-3 (hbk)
ISBN: 978-1-032-36494-0 (pbk)
ISBN: 978-1-003-33227-5 (ebk)

DOI: 10.4324/9781003332275

Typeset in Bembo
by MPS Limited, Dehradun

CONTENTS

Notes on the Author	x
List of Contributors	xi
Foreword	xii
Executive Summary	xiv
List of Abbreviations	xviii

Introduction	1

PART I
The Rise of Religion in Development – Background and Current Trends — 7

1. Religion Matters – Rediscovering Religion — 9
2. The Sustainable Development Goals and Religion – The Rise of Faith Actors in Development — 17
3. Meet the Family – Religion's Different Faces in Development — 25
4. What's So Special about Them? Potentials and Problems of Faith Actors in Development — 33

PART II
Religion and the SDGs 43

5 "It Is Not God's Will for Us to Be Poor!" Religion Matters for Poverty Alleviation (SDG 1 and 2) 45

   SPOTLIGHT: A CHRISTIAN PERSPECTIVE ON PENTECOSTAL POVERTY ALLEVIATION IN SOUTH AFRICA (PETER WHITE)

6 "Holistic Healing" – Religion Matters for Good Health and Well-Being (SDG 3) 54

   SPOTLIGHT: MULTI-RELIGIOUS PERSPECTIVES ON RESPONDING TO THE COVID-19 PANDEMIC (AZZA KARAM)

7 "Largest and Most Successful Education Provider ... Outside of Public Education Systems" – Religion Matters for Quality Education (SDG 4) 65

   SPOTLIGHT: A BUDDHIST PERSPECTIVE ON WISDOM AND HUMAN VALUES IN EDUCATION IN MALAYSIA (WENDY YEE MEI TIEN)

8 "Your Women, Let Them Be Silent in the Assemblies" – Religion Matters for Gender Equality (SDG 5) 75

   SPOTLIGHT: A MUSLIM PERSPECTIVE ON GENDER EQUALITY AND VIOLENCE AGAINST WOMEN AND GIRLS (VAWG) (SANDRA IMAN PERTEK)

9 "I Have a Dream" – Religion Matters for the Reduction of Inequality (SDG 10) 84

   SPOTLIGHT: A JEWISH PERSPECTIVE ON DEMOCRACY AND MINORITY RIGHTS IN ISRAEL (PAULINE KOLLONTAI)

10 "Green Religion" – Religion Matters for Climate Action (SDG 13) 92

   SPOTLIGHT: AN INDIGENOUS PERSPECTIVE ON TRADITIONAL ECOLOGICAL KNOWLEDGE AND CLIMATE CHANGE (JOHN C. RODWAN)

11 "Brokers of Peace" – Religion Matters for Peace and
   Justice (SDG 16)   102
   SPOTLIGHT: A CHRISTIAN PERSPECTIVE ON RECONCILIATION
   AND FORGIVENESS AFTER THE RWANDAN GENOCIDE
   (CHRISTOPHE MBONYINGABO)

12 Now What? Implications for Academics, Policymakers, and
   Practitioners   112

References   *118*
Index   *132*

NOTES ON THE AUTHOR

Christine Schliesser is a Senior Lecturer for Systematic Theology and Ethics at Zurich University and Director of Studies at the Center for Faith & Society at Fribourg University, Switzerland. She is also a Research Fellow in Studies in Historical Trauma and Transformation at Stellenbosch University, South Africa. Coming from the perspective of Christian theology and ethics, she has a sustained interest in the role of theology and religion in the public sphere ("Public Theology"), and in particular in sustainable development. Christine Schliesser furthermore explores the role of religious actors in national reconciliation processes after historical trauma such as in Rwanda and South Africa. Next to peace and reconciliation studies, she focuses in her work on the theology and ethics of Dietrich Bonhoeffer. Together with Pauline Kollontai and Ayse Kadayifci-Orellana, she co-edits the Routledge book series, *Religion Matters. On the Significance of Religion in Global Issues*. Her recent publications include *Alternative Approaches in Conflict Resolution* (eds. Christine Schliesser and Martin Leiner, Palgrave Macmillan 2018) and *Religion Matters – On the Significance of Religion in Conflict and Conflict Resolution* (with Pauline Kollontai and Ayse Kadayifci-Orellana, Routledge Press 2021).

CONTRIBUTORS

Azza Karam is Secretary General of Religions for Peace, the largest global multi-religious coalition of religious institutions and faith leaders. She is also a Professor of Religion and Development at the Vrije Universiteit of Amsterdam, the Netherlands.

Pauline Kollontai is a Professor Emerita of Higher Education in Theology and Religious Studies at York St John University, UK. She is a Fellow of the UK's Higher Education Academy and a member of the Centre for Theological Inquiry, Princeton, USA.

Christophe Mbonyingabo is a Rwandan sociologist. He is the founder and director of Christian Action for Reconciliation and Social Assistance (CARSA), an FBO dedicated to reconciling and supporting genocide perpetrators and survivors.

Wendy Yee Mei Tien is an Associate Professor at the University of Malaya. She specialises in Youth Studies (Inter-Ethnic Relations), Peace Building, and Intercultural Dialogue. She is an International Fellow of KAICIID (King Abdullah bin Abdulaziz International Centre for Interreligious and Intercultural Dialogue).

Sandra Iman Pertek is an ESRC Postdoctoral Fellow at the University of Birmingham, UK, and a gender and social development practitioner with expertise in violence against women and faith with over a decade's experience in humanitarian and international development settings.

John C. Rodwan is a US citizen with lifelong residence in the Great Lakes region of the Midwest. He is the director of an environmental department for a Native American tribe residing within their traditional homeland.

Peter White is a Senior Lecturer in the Department of Practical Theology and Missiology in the Faculty of Theology at Stellenbosch University and a pastor in the Christ Apostolic Church International (CACI).

FOREWORD

On September 16, 2022, Mahsa Amini, a young Iranian woman, died in police custody in Iran, after having been arrested by the morality police, who accused her of wearing her head covering improperly. In view of the ensuing protests in Iran against the Mullah regime, the German minister of foreign affairs Annalena Baerbock stated two weeks later in the German parliament: The terror of the Iranian moral guardians "has nothing, but nothing at all, to do with religion or culture" (Baerbock 2022, translation is mine). This is not only a dangerous error, but it also shows an alarming lack of religious literacy, i.e. the ability to understand, analyse, and interpret the religious dimensions in a given context.

Religion matters. And this is exactly why my colleagues Pauline Kollontai and Ayse Kadayifci-Orellana and myself launched the series "Religion Matters. On the Significance of Religion for Global Issues" in 2020. We are convinced that religion matters not only in private and personal lives, but also in the public sphere. It matters in how we tackle the challenges we are facing today as global citizens, including conflict, climate change, and health. The Agenda 2030 with the 17 Sustainable Development Goals (SDGs) at its heart serve as a frame of orientation for the different volumes of this series as each one explores the role of religion in a given issue. Not only does this series explore the – ever-ambivalent – role of religion, but it also includes concrete implications for academics, policymakers, and practitioners on how to better understand and include the constructive resources that religion offers and how to deal with its more problematic features.

This volume serves as the introduction to the series by giving an orientation as to how exactly religion matters for the SDGs. Based on our firm conviction that not one religion or discipline can do it alone, I am grateful to the following guest writers, who contributed the wisdom and experiences from their respective faith traditions and cultural backgrounds on a particular SDG. Thank you Azza Karam, Pauline Kollontai, Christophe Mbonyingabo, Sandra Iman Pertek, John C. Rodwan,

Wendy Yee Mei Tien, and Peter White! Your insights are invaluable. And I am particularly thankful to my editor colleague Pauline Kollontai for offering super helpful comments on the manuscript. Thanks so much, Pauline! I am very pleased that we could secure collaboration with the Swiss artist duo Manuel Dürr and Taco Hammacher (aka Schwarzfalter), who contribute the amazing covers for our series. Merci vielmal, Mändu, and Taco! And thank you also to my students. I have tested and tried each argument that made it into this volume with them first. One of the goals of this series is to be as easily accessible as possible, which today means Open Access. I therefore thank the Swiss National Science Foundation (SNSF) for their financial support of the Open Access version of this volume. A further warm thank you is extended to Dr Lee-Anne Roux for her wonderful support with the editorial process. I also express my sincere thanks to Routledge, namely Ceri McLardy and Iman Hakimi, for their excellent collaboration. The ultimate thanks goes to my husband Benjamin Schliesser and our children Naemi Joy, Chira Jael, and Noel Benjamin.

Christine Schliesser,
Gals, November 2022

EXECUTIVE SUMMARY

For 85% of the people on this planet (World Population Review 2022), religion is a relevant factor, influencing not only the way they think, but also how they act. For achieving the great vision of the Agenda 2030 with the 17 SDGs at its heart, collaboration with faith-based actors is therefore not an option, but a necessity. From the analysis and discussion, the following implications result for academics, policymakers, and practitioners engaged in development theory and practice, faith-based and secular alike.

Implication 1: Beyond the Binary – Bridging the Religious-Secular Divide

"There is now indisputable and solid evidence that religions and religious actors can successfully be invited into, and contribute to global development" (Udenrigsministeriet 2019: 6). In spite of this evidence referred to by the Danish Ministry of Foreign Affairs, collaborations between faith-based and secular actors in development are still far from being mainstreamed. At the same time, religious engagement for the sake of religious engagement is not enough. Rather, "there must be a commitment to better religious engagement – real SRE [strategic religious engagement], … i.e. purposeful, self-aware, unrepetitive/ duplicative" (Wilkinson 2021: 82) Religion matters for the SDGs – this insight must become the premise for development theory and practice.

Implication 2: Reading Religion Right – Seven Dimensions of Religion

The "religious factor" in development often remains vague and difficult to grasp, and there is "an ongoing need for shared analytical and definitional clarity when dealing with religion in development processes" (UNFPA 2014: 52). For that matter, even for faith-based actors themselves it can be difficult to explain their unique contributions. This book introduces a seven-dimensional analytical model designed to help academics, policymakers, and practitioners recognise, analyse, and interpret the religious dimensions within a given context appropriately. These seven dimensions of religion are religion as religio-scape, community, teachings, spirituality, practice, institutions, and framework (see Chapter 5).

Implication 3: Creating Spaces of Trust – The Need for Encounter Between All Relevant Actors

"Creating forums for interfaith and secular-religious debate on international development is an important step in understanding and respecting differences, as well as finding and pursuing shared goals" (Social Science Research Council [SSRC] 2011: 26). This recommendation which resulted from a series of consultations on religion, development, and the United Nations (UN) in 2011 has not lost any of its validity, nor urgency. We need spaces of trust where all relevant actors in development, including academics, policymakers, and practitioners – both faith-based and secular – can encounter one another, build trust, and share insights and information.

Implication 4: Bilinguality – Religious and Developmental Literacy

In order to mitigate the Babylonian confusion that inevitably arises in international, interdisciplinary and cross-sectional settings like development work, all partners involved need to become bilingual, or more precisely, multilingual. Bilinguality here does not only refer to the semantics of a language. Rather, faith-based actors need to acquire development literacy, such as human rights language, while secular actors need skills in religious literacy, in order to "learn their [faith-based actors'] 'language' and culture" (UNFPA 2014: 51).

Implication 5: Theology Matters – Why We Need Immanent Critics

Learning human rights language is not enough for faith-based actors. Rather, the very idea of universal human rights needs to be made at home in each and every single faith tradition. Otherwise, human rights – and the SDGs that arose from this very concept – will always be in danger of remaining on the surface only. For the SDGs to become an integral part of everyone's DNA, we need theologians who speak critically, and self-critically, from within their own faith traditions. These immanent critics, who do the crucial work of connecting their own faith tradition with the concerns of human rights and the SDGs, need to be supported.

Implication 6: Women in Focus – Rethinking Religious Leadership

Much work has been done on the importance of engaging religious leaders for sustainable development work. And rightly so. Yet engaging religious leaders oftentimes means engaging older men. This does not only lead to a gender-imbalanced representation of religious communities within the field of development, but effectively ignores the wisdom, insights and experiences of the very people who work in all areas of development every day – women of faith. This leads to two consequences, namely (1) the concept of 'religious leadership' needs to be reconsidered, and (2) the criteria for the engagement of faith-based actors in development need to be adapted to better incorporate the voice of women.

Implication 7: Youth in Focus – And What About Social Media?

The importance of engaging the youth for sustainable development is undisputed, especially against the background that many of the less developed countries have a much greater proportion of young people as compared to so-called developed countries. It is therefore all the more surprising that social media, which is one of the most effective tools for reaching the youth, remains underutilized. Development actors must become more efficient in employing social media for outreach to the youth on matters of faith and development.

Implication 8: What Good Is This? – Accountability and Measuring Impact

The road to coordination between donors, multilaterals, and faith-based organisations (FBOs) must include accountability, for instance, by means of clear action plans including guidelines and timelines. "Accountability will be key in the move towards action" (UNFPA 2016: 41). At the same time, more work needs to be invested in the development of methods and frameworks for evaluation and impact measurement. This is necessary not only for strengthening the projects and initiatives in the field, but also for professional recognition as well as for the communication and engagement with policymakers. Although recent years have seen improvement (cf. Garred, Hume & Herrington 2021), much more remains to be done.

Implication 9: One Faith Is Not Enough – The Power of Multifaith Engagement

"Ambitious goals and complex problems can best be tackled when different faith communities work together" (Religions for Peace 2022: n.p.). This holds especially true in the complexities of the field of global development. Two implications follow, one for secular development actors and the other one for faith-based actors. (1) Collaboration with faith-based actors often means focussing on the three Abrahamic religions – Judaism, Christianity, and Islam. The insights and wisdom of other faith traditions, including the indigenous and dharmic traditions, should also be taken into consideration. (2) Faith-based actors need to collaborate not only with secular actors but also with each other, developing multi-religious narratives and engagements on the SDGs.

LIST OF ABBREVIATIONS

ATR	African Traditional Religion
BLHDL	Basic Law on Human Dignity and Liberty
CACI	Christ Apostolic Church International
CAFOD	Catholic Agency for Overseas Development
CARSA	Christian Action for Reconciliation and Social Assistance
CCP	Chinese Communist Party
CLJC	Constitution, Law, and Justice Commission
CPCE	Communion of Protestant Churches in Europe
CSI	Christian Solidarity International
DDVE	Development Dialogue on Values and Ethics
DSDG	Division for Sustainable Development Goal
FBHP	Faith-Based Health Provider
FBO	Faith-Based Organisation
FGM	Female Genital Mutilation
GBV	Gender-Based Violence
GDP	Gross Domestic Product
GOP	Greek Orthodox Patriarchate
GSDR	Global Sustainable Development Report
HDI	Human Development Index
HIPC	Heavily Indebted Poor Countries
HLPF	High-Level Political Forum
IATF	Inter-Agency Task Force
ICRC	International Committee of the Red Cross
INGO	International Non-Governmental Organisation
IRC	Interreligious Council
ISIS	Islamic State of Iraq and Syria
ISKCON	International Society for Krishna Consciousness

List of Abbreviations

JLI	Joint Learning Initiative on Faith & Local Communities
KAICIID	King Abdullah bin Abdulaziz International Centre for Interreligious and Intercultural Dialogue
MDG	Millennium Development Goal
MENA	Middle East and North Africa
NGO	Non-Governmental Organisation
NHRI	National Human Rights Institution
OSCE	Organisation for Security and Co-operation
PaRD	International Partnership on Religion and Sustainable Development
PBUH	Peace Be Upon Him
RaD	Religions and Development
RfP	Religions for Peace
RHR	Rabbis for Human Rights
RNGO	Religious Non-Governmental Organisation
SBC	Southern Baptist Convention
SDG	Sustainable Development Goal
SRE	Strategic Religious Engagement
SSRC	Social Science Research Council
StatsSA	Statistics South Africa
TBA	Traditional Birth Assistant
TM	Tag-Meir
UDHR	Universal Declaration of Human Rights
UNDESA	United Nations Department of Economic and Social Affairs
UNDP	United Nations Development Programme
UNESCO	United Nations Educational, Scientific, and Cultural Organisation
UNFCCC	United Nations Framework Convention on Climate Change
UNFPA	United Nations Population Fund
UNIATF	UN Interagency Task Force
UN IATF-R	Interagency Task Force on Engaging Religion and Sustainable Development
UNICEF	United Nations International Children's Emergency Fund
USOIRF	United States Office of International Religious Freedom
VAWG	Violence against Women and Girls
WCC	World Council of Churches
WCED	World Commission on Environment and Development
WFDD	World Faiths Development Dialogue
WHO	World Health Organisation
WIR	World Inequality Report

INTRODUCTION

Religion Matters: Religion and the SDGs

More than eight out of ten people. This is the number of people worldwide who profess adherence to a faith tradition. In fact, the exact number is 85% in 2022 (World Population Review 2022), with an upward trend, making faith communities the largest transnational civil society actors. Religion and its institutions such as temples, churches, or mosques are as old as humanity itself. No other force known to human culture is older, rooted deeper in the human collective consciousness, or is able to connect humans with one another more extensively. Up to this day, religion is a reality for the vast majority of the people on this planet. And this reality shapes how people think, how they act – and not act. Add to this the fact that concepts such as justice, peace, love, and solidarity are at home in virtually all faith traditions. For ages, faith actors have been feeding the hungry, tending to the sick, and taking care of society's marginalised. In short, faith actors have been active in development work before the term "development" itself was even coined. Along with the Joint Learning Initiative on Faith & Local Communities (JLI), I use the term "development" "as shorthand for all the socially oriented work that religions might undertake to improve or protect dignity, society, and wellbeing" (JLI 2022: 13).

And this work continues to this day. A 2016 United Nations Population Fund (UNFPA) report points out

> In many African countries facing severe shortages and poor distribution of health workers, faith based organizations (FBOs) provide between 30%–70% of health care services. Moreover, FBO facilities often serve remote and rural areas where governments have the greatest difficulty in attracting and retaining health workers. Yet FBO health workers frequently remain under recognized for their contributions and uncounted in national statistics.

> Members of FBO networks also provide a significant amount of preservice education and in service health worker training in African countries. In Malawi and Uganda, for example, FBOs provide 70% of nursing and midwifery training; in Tanzania and Zambia they provide between 30% and 55% of such training. FBO schools have a history of management flexibility and innovation and an excellent track record of training health workers that serve in rural areas.
>
> (UNFPA 2016: 4)

So clearly, religion matters for development and the SDGs. The past few years have seen increasing recognition of this, demonstrated not least by the fact that the "amount of evidence for faith activity and contributions in the development and humanitarian spheres has increased over the last decade" (JLI 2022: 11). Yet just as clearly, religion is ambivalent (Appleby 2000). Religion – any religion – can be used for good *and* for bad. For example, for uniting people for peace and reconciliation, and for inciting hatred and violence. For rallying for gender equality, and for preventing girls from attaining higher education. And one more thing is clear, namely the notorious unclarity of religion. While the "religious factor", for example, within a given conflict situation, seems obvious, the precise nature of this "religious factor" remains oftentimes vague and nebulous. This makes religion a somewhat uneasy factor in the development equation, to say the least.

Religion and the SDGs: The What's, the Who's, and the How's

What? This book brings all three of these aspects into the picture, namely, (1) religion matters for the SDGs, (2) religion is inherently ambivalent, and (3) religion needs to be analysed properly. This may appear somewhat presumptuous for one short book. Granted. And this is why this book is merely an introductory volume for an entire series – *Religion Matters. On the Significance of Religion in Global Issues* – that is dedicated to the analysis of the role of religion in the SDGs. Our planet and we as global citizens are faced with numerous challenges today ranging from ending poverty and climate action to peace and justice for all. And we need to look at each of these challenges carefully and the role of religion therein. This book does not pretend to deliver an in-depth and comprehensive analysis of the impact of religion on every single SDG. If you are looking for this, please consult one of the specific volumes in this series or ask a bookseller of your confidence. What this book aims to do, however, is provide an introduction into why religion matters for the SDGs and how it matters. It is meant to whet your appetite. In order to do so, it provides insights into the background and current trends of religion in development and then takes 7 of the 17 SDGs to illustrate why and how religion matters. These seven goals are chosen because they are among the more prominent SDGs, such as ending hunger and poverty (SDGs 1 and 2), gender equality (SDG 5), or climate action (SDG 13).

Who? The topic of discussion, "religion and development", necessitates a multilateral approach in several respects. The complexity of the challenges addressed by the SDGs calls for the collaboration of *all* relevant actors, including academics, policymakers, and practitioners. And it calls for the united wisdom from people representing different disciplines, geographical and cultural backgrounds, and faith traditions. While the descriptive and analytical parts of this book are written by its main author, who comes from a Christian, central European perspective, the discussion of each particular SDG always includes a *spotlight* on a particular topic from a guest author representing a different context. For example, the general analysis of the role of religion in climate action (SDG 13) is illustrated by an indigenous perspective on traditional ecological knowledge. When speaking of the "who's" of this book, one more aspect is important. All the voices contributing to this book are insider voices. This means that the authors are at home within their respective faith traditions – they live and love their faith. This does not mean they are blind to their own tradition's shortcomings. Rather, they all speak as immanent critics, i.e. as people of faith who critically and self-critically engage with their own faith tradition. But why not ask authors with a neutral and objective point of view? Two main reasons. Firstly, it would defy the very purpose of this book and series, namely exploring the role of religion in the SDGs, to exclude faith actors from presenting their specific insights. Secondly, we don't believe in the possibility of absolute neutrality or objectivity. This post-Enlightenment postulation has been accepted for far too long without questioning by the academic world and beyond. If post-modernity teaches us one thing, it is that none of us is a clean slate, but we all bring our experiences, our context, and our worldviews that shape who we are and how we think, to the epistemological table. Rather than pretending to be value-free, we need to be transparent about our own particular perspective. It is this transparency that fosters critical and self-critical engagement with one's own tradition. This in turn enables genuine tolerance towards and engagement with other faith and non-faith traditions.

How? Secular actors have repeatedly voiced the "ongoing need for shared analytical and definitional clarity when dealing with religion in development processes" (UNFPA 2014: 52). This sentiment, by the way, is shared by faith actors as well, many of whom have difficulties in describing precisely the unique contributions of their faith tradition in a given development context. Different models and methods have been introduced for the analysis of religion, some more useful than others. This book utilises a seven-dimensional analytical model of religion that is simple without being simplistic. This model was originally created to better understand the role of religion in different conflict settings (Frazer & Friedli 2015; Frazer & Owen 2018). In order to use it for development in general, it has been modified to fit this screen, so to speak. Reading religion right becomes easier for academics, policymakers, and practitioners if they are aware of the seven different faces of religion: Religion as religio-scape, community, teachings, spirituality, practice, institutions, and framework (cf. Chapter 5). These dimensions elucidate the different roles of religion in a given context, what exactly it is that faith actors contribute, how the constructive resources of religion can be harnessed more effectively, and how its problematic features can be better understood and addressed. At the same time, analysis is not all there is. As humans, we are storytelling animals (Gottschall 2013). We make sense of our reality through stories – we live in our stories; we are our stories. Understanding the role of a faith tradition in a given context therefore means listening to the "powerful and touching stories" of people (UNFPA 2016: 42). The guest authors invited to contribute to this volume share their own unique stories. Linking analysis with real-life illustrations, and theory with practical experiences, facilitates a more holistic understanding of the interconnectedness of religion and the SDGs.

But What Exactly Is Religion?

The impossibility to find, much less agree on a common definition of religion has become almost a methodological dogma itself in the field of religious studies (Wilson 1998). Debates are usually framed between substantial understandings of religion, i.e. referring to religion's content or dogma, vs. functional conceptions of religion, i.e. relating to the functions of religion such as creating identities or insiders vs. outsiders. For the questions tackled in this book, these discussions are rather fruitless. Instead, it has been found most helpful to employ a pragmatic understanding of religion (cf. Waardenburg 1986: 250–255). This means that whatever interlocutors and communities describe and understand as religion, is described and understood as religion in this book. In development contexts, different terms exist for speaking about religious actors and their organisations. The one term that seems to have won the race is "faith-based organisation" (FBO). At the same time, the concept of FBOs – be they large, formal, and international, or small-scale and local – does not capture the whole range of actors involved. A recent study on religion and the SDGs therefore rightly proposes the term "faith actors" as the overarching concept (Tomalin et al. 2019: 105). While the term "faith actors" incorporates FBOs, it also includes religious individuals such as religious leaders, who increasingly come into focus as valuable cooperation partners in promoting the SDGs. Furthermore, faith actors can refer to religious communities that are located structurally between an individual and a formal organisation. Such groups may centre around places of worship such as mosques or churches, yet may also evolve – and dissolve – spontaneously around a certain issue or agenda.

What Lies Ahead: Outline of This Book

This book, and the series it introduces, seeks to build bridges across the secular-religious divide and between the different spheres of engagement in development, including academics, policymakers, and practitioners. To this end, this book – and all volumes in this series, for that matter – begin with an executive summary and end with practical implications and recommendations. In between, this book consists of two main parts. Part I provides an overview of the rise of religion in development, sketching out background information and exploring current trends. The seven-dimensional analytical model of religion is introduced here, and the potentials and problems of faith actors in development are explored further. Part II combines description with analysis as seven SDGs are being discussed in detail: "No Poverty" (SDG 1) and "Zero Hunger" (SDG 2), "Good Health and Well-Being" (SDG 3), "Quality Education" (SDG 4), "Gender Equality" (SDG 5), "Reduced Inequalities" (SDG 10), "Climate Action" (SDG 13), and "Peace, Justice and Strong Institutions" (SDG 16) (cf. United Nations. Department of Economic and Social Affairs [UNDESA] n.d.). Here, the seven-dimensional model is put to the test as the impact of religion and the concrete contributions of faith actors are being analysed. Each discussion of an SDG is illustrated by a specific spotlight written by one of the guest authors, contributing a different perspective in terms of faith tradition, discipline, and geographical and cultural context.

The successful implementation of the Agenda 2030 with the 17 SDGs at its centre requires nothing less than a paradigm change of hearts and minds. This in turn requires the joint collaboration of all relevant actors, secular and faith-based, academics, policymakers, and practitioners alike. The methodological approach of this book thus mirrors the conviction that if we indeed care to cooperate, the potential for change is phenomenal.

> *I have long believed that when governments and civil society work towards a common goals, transformational change is possible. Faiths and religions are a central part of that equation.*
>
> (Ban Ki-Moon, cited in SSRC 2012: ii)

PART I

The Rise of Religion in Development – Background and Current Trends

PART

I

Lake Selection,
Development Strategies, and
Current Trends

1
RELIGION MATTERS – REDISCOVERING RELIGION

The Death of God in the West

Religion has never truly left us. Not even in the West, where the Enlightenment has dethroned the gods and clergy in favour of pure reason. In the wake of the rise of reason, philosophers and even theologians have pronounced the end of all religion and the death of God. Yet during the centuries, the focus of the criticism of religion changed. While the early criticism of religion was directed primarily at the claim of the Christian church to exclusivity in explaining and interpreting the world and the cosmos, the 18th century refocused the centre of criticism towards the Christian monopoly of an ethical way of life. This again gave way in the 19th century as the social function of (again mostly Christian) religion became the centre of criticism. Religion came to be seen as a means of satisfied self-appeasement, of heteronomy, and of safeguarding power structures that needed to be identified and overcome. Coming from a different perspective, yet joined in the deconstruction of religion, thinkers like Ludwig Feuerbach, Sigmund Freud, and Karl Marx created theories that not only did not need religion but helped to set the framework for an atheistic point of view. With the continuing advance of natural sciences, the renunciation of transcendental foundations became the solely accepted methodological premise for the acquisition of knowledge.

While the criticism of religion gnawed away on the philosophical, cultural, and ethical authority of (the Christian) religion as the once sole interpreter of life and death, the developments following the Enlightenment also cast a new social role for religion. When the French people revolted against the tyranny of their kings, church, and clergy, the role of religion itself became collateral damage. Far from its once prominent role in the public sphere, religion became relegated to the private realm. Religious matters thus became a matter of personal taste that had to have no bearings on discussions in the public sphere. Quite on the contrary, when discussing matters of public relevance, religiously based arguments have since been sidelined. This view has been prominently pushed by the philosophical school of political liberalism since the 1970s, with John Rawls as its most well-known representative (Rawls 1993). His concept of a "public reason" in debates on major public issues permits only arguments that would allow all reasonable people to generally agree on and therefore excludes any arguments derived from particular comprehensive worldviews such as religions. Rawls' thoughts have had a profound influence on the way we discuss public, let alone global issues such as justice, peace, or climate change. Rawls' claims have sparked a lively discussion as they met with resistance from different perspectives, not least from theology. In view of the right to religious freedom, theologian Jeffrey Stout criticises the (self-) limitations called for by Rawls: "Rawls seems to be saying that while the right to express our religious commitments freely is guaranteed twice over in the Bill of Rights, this is not a right of which we ought make essential use in the centre of the political arena, where the most important questions are decided" (Stout 2005: 68).

Yet even before Rawls, religion sociologist Max Weber (1994: 12) famously pronounced the "disenchantment of the world" ("Entzauberung der Welt"). Together with the post-Enlightenment relegation of religion to the private realm, Weber's dictum has for decades presided over the discourses in (Western) politics, societies, and academics. In its own sphere of influence, communism has done a clean job in eradicating religion as the much-dreaded "opiate of the people" (Karl Marx). Even after the end of the Cold War in 1989 and until this very day, countries that had been under the influence of the Socialist regime, such as former East Germany or Albania, are more or less religious waste lands. In former East Germany, so the saying goes, people have forgotten about religion to the degree that they have even forgotten what it is that they forgot. Not to mention current communist countries such as China and North Korea that seem entirely disinterested in religion.

Rediscovering Religion

Yet this is not the whole story. For some time now, it has become apparent that the so-called "secularisation thesis" has failed. This thesis – wrongly – assumes that modern societies would become ever more secular as the functions of religion are increasingly being taken over by other societal actors. While it might be a bit rash to speak of the "desecularisation of the world" (ed. Berger 1999), recent years have certainly seen "a renewed interest in questions of religiosity and its role in the making of 'modern' society" (Long 2012: vii). The perceived renewed interest in religion is both supported and enforced by empirical research. The numbers show that religions are growing everywhere around the world – with the notable exception of Western Europe and North America. These are the places, however, where much of global political decision-making is taking place – with the UN headquarters being based in New York City, for example – not least concerning issues of global development. It seems that Western Europe and North America, being areas of religion's decline, have long turned a blind eye on religion's presence in other parts of the globe.

Both the decline of religion in parts of the world and the growth of religion in other parts are significantly influenced by demographic factors. Members of a religion are generally younger and have more children than people who do not belong to a religious group. Christian women, for example, have an overall birth rate of 2.6. Yet it is much lower in Europe, where from 2010 to 2015 almost 6 million more Christians died than were being born (Hackett & McClendon 2017; cf. Sherwood 2018). While Christianity is currently still the largest religion in the world (2.3 billion or 31% of the world's population of 7.3 billion), Islam is the fastest growing religion. With 1.8 billion Muslims (or 24% of the world population) and a birth rate of 2.9 children per Muslim woman, the world's Muslim population is expected to increase by 70% until 2060, overtaking Christianity as the largest religion by the middle of the 21st century. The third largest group, namely 1.2 billion people or 16% of the world's population, does not have any religious affiliations. From this it does not necessarily follow that everyone in this group is a committed atheist. Many do have a sense of spirituality, yet they are not members of an institutionalised religion. Hindus make up the fourth largest group and the third largest religion with 1.1 billion followers, which equal about 15% of the world's population. With about 500 million or almost 7%, Buddhism is the next largest religion. Among the larger world religions, Buddhism is the only one that is going to experience a 7% decline in numbers, according to the data analysed. Folk or traditional religions comprise the next group that amounts to a total of 400 million or 6% of the global population. Sikhism, Bahá'í, and Jainism are lesser practiced religions that together have about 58 million followers (below 1%). Judaism has 14 million adherents, which is 0.2% of the world's population (Pew Research Center 2015). Yet while demographics are one major aspect in the projected development of religion, there are other factors as well such as conversion. This will be discussed in more detail below in the context of religious growth in China.

In general, almost every religion comes in different denominations or subgroups. Roman Catholicism is the largest denomination of Christianity, with about 1.3 billion members. Next to Catholics, there are Protestants, Russian Orthodox, Greek Orthodox, Anglicans, Baptists, Mennonites, and many more. Islam is divided into the largest group of Sunni, Shia Ibadi, Ahmadiyya, or Sufi. For Hinduism, there are four main strands, namely Vaishnavism, Shaivism, Shaktism, and Smartism. Buddhism then encompasses the Theravada and the Mahayana traditions, while Jews can be Orthodox or ultra-Orthodox, Conservative, or Reform.

In addition, geography plays a role when considering the topic of religion. The most religious region in the world and, at the same time, the most populous, is Asia-Pacific (Sherwood 2018). Around 99% of the world's Hindus and Buddhists, and 90% of those who adhere to folk or traditional religions, call this region their home. A further noteworthy point is that 75% of religious people live in a country where their own religion is the majority religion. 75% of all Muslims, for example, live in countries where Islam is the main religion. 87% of Christians live in

Christian-majority countries, while 97% of Hindus live in Hindu-majority countries, namely India, Mauritius, and Nepal. Only Buddhists live mostly (72%) in a country where Buddhism is in the minority.

The Formerly and the Not Religious – What About Europe and China?

There are voices, particularly in the West, arguing that people in general are becoming less religious. German Islam scientist Thomas Bauer, for instance, contends that recent years have revealed a tendency towards fundamentalism that goes along with a tendency to become indifferent in the face of religion (Bauer 2018). Both tendencies, according to Bauer, are inclined to erode traditional religion. On the one hand, Bauer's observations are persuasive. His historical analysis of Europe shows that this continent for many centuries had been one of the least diverse areas worldwide (Bauer 2018: 9ff.). In Europe, Christianity had led to a rather homogeneous religious landscape with comparatively few members of other religions such as Judaism or Islam. These historical roots play a role in creating what Bauer describes as the current absence of true polyphony and ambiguity. In the religious sphere, this has, on the one hand, led to the rise of seemingly simple, straightforward answers to complex challenges as provided by fundamentalism. On the other hand, increasing indifference to religious matters describes the mirroring manoeuvre to circumvent dealing with different and competing voices. While the empirical data referenced above supports Bauer's observations and his historical-cultural interpretation of a retreat of traditional or institutionalised religion in Europe, his analysis does not hold up to the developments in other regions of the world. When it comes to religion, Europe is the exception, not the rule – and at the same time, Europe itself is still Christian, increasingly Muslim, secular, pluralistic, and everything at once. So while on the one hand, Christianity as Europe's main traditional and institutionalised religion is retreating in Europe, there is nevertheless a growing awareness of the role of religion in global issues. International development is a prime example of this, as we will come to see (cf. Chapter 2). Against this background, the renewed interest in the role of religion as visible in Europe and North America is a concept that "has more relevance in the Global North than South, since in many settings in the Global South, secularism never took hold or was not as widespread as in the North" (Tomalin, Haustein & Kidy 2019: 107).

Yet how about China? As a growing empire ready to challenge the United States' status as the world's number one superpower, China seems entirely disinterested in religion. Or rather, to be more precise, China is interested in religion primarily in terms of ensuring that the religions which are practiced in China are well controlled and monitored to ensure they have no significant influence in the public sphere and in politics. The numbers speak for themselves: With a population of about 1.44 billion people, already today about every fifth person on this planet is Chinese (in 2100, however, India is expected to overtake China as the country with the most inhabitants). For decades, China's officials have followed an expressively atheist agenda. While East Asia is, on the one hand, the most religious area worldwide, it is at the same time hosting the largest number of people (76%) not claiming affiliations with any religion, 700 million of which are Chinese. Yet this seems to represent only one side of the story. In the past four decades, China has witnessed a religious revival, with most of the new believers committing themselves to Christianity. While China officially recognises five religions – Buddhism, Catholicism, Daoism, Islam, and Protestantism – it is Chinese Protestantism that has been experiencing the strongest increase with a 10% annual growth since 1979 (Albert 2018). Some estimate that by 2030 China might have the largest population of Christians. Christianity in China is partly state-sanctioned – as the three major bodies, the Three-Self Patriotic Movement, the China Christian Council, and the Chinese Patriotic Catholic Association – and partly underground, mostly in the form of house churches. Both forms, official and unofficial, have been experiencing an increase in membership across regions and demographics. Analysing the reasons behind the surge of religion in atheist China, social scientists point to a perceived rise of a spiritual vacuum in the wake of unprecedented economic growth. The ideology of the officially atheist Chinese Communist Party (CCP) is losing traction, while Protestantism appeals with its sense of fellowship and solidarity and its moral system. Faced with the unexpected rise in religion, China's leadership is wary. "Faith-based organizations are perceived as one of the most serious threats to the Communist party", says Fenggang Yang (cited in Albert 2018: n.p.), leading to growing repression against religious groups in general and Christians in particular.

Does Religion Really Matter?

It certainly does. And it does so in many different ways because religion is inherently ambivalent. This means both its dark and its light sides can be used for many different purposes. One of the most obvious examples of how religion matters is religion's role in conflict. Examples come to mind quickly and range from past conflicts, such as the Crusades and the 30 Years War, to more recent conflicts including the Northern Ireland conflict, and the Islamic State of Iraq and Syria (ISIS) and Boko Haram insurgencies, to name but a few. Religion is holistic in the sense that it affects the person in her/his entirety. Religion shapes how we think, how we perceive ourselves, each other and our surroundings, and how we act. It is therefore not surprising that religion matters in virtually every sphere of life, not least in politics. Donald Trump's victory in the presidential elections in 2016, for example, was owed not least to the staunch support of evangelical Christians. Or take Poland's and Hungary's anti-migration politics. Prime Minister of Hungary Viktor Orbán justifies his country's stance against migrants by pointing to the need to protect his people and his country's "Christian culture".

Yet while religion can be employed for seemingly any conflict-driving, negative end, it also holds numerous and potent resources for justice, peace, and solidarity. Religion, for instance, can play a central role in conflict resolution.

14   The Rise of Religion in Development

Numerous case studies attest to the potency of religion in different contexts as the following examples demonstrate (cf. Schliesser et al. 2021: 77–90). Christian churches are significant actors for social healing in post-genocide Rwanda, just as the Jewish Holy Scriptures inspire Jewish human rights activists in negotiating land rights conflicts in Israel and Palestine. Civil society initiatives such as PAIMAN demonstrate the effective and sustainable peace-making efforts of Muslim women in Pakistan. Religious actors of all faith traditions across the world are instrumental for countless social projects. Synagogues, churches, mosques, and other religious institutions help provide food and shelter for the needy. The most recent refugee crisis sweeping Europe since 2015 and compounded by the war in Ukraine has brought forward countless religiously motivated volunteers, engaging in projects ranging from civil sea rescue missions over church asylum up to free language classes.

Rising awareness of how religion affects decision-making and life choices on a personal and collective level results in an increase of attention and resources devoted to this issue not only from the side of practitioners and academics, but also from policymakers. Governments in secularised Western countries have begun to establish different formats with the aim of facilitating a better understanding of the impact of religion in public and global issues. One example of a transnational initiative is the European Union's appointment of a Special Envoy for the promotion of freedom of religion or belief outside the EU in 2016. At the same time, national governments have set up different bodies with a focus on religion. Based on the insight that traditional foreign policy between nation states needs to be supplemented by a foreign policy between societies in order to be more inclusive of impulses from civil society, the German government set up a task force on Religion and Foreign Policy in 2018. This followed a task force on Responsibility of Religions for Peace, which looked specifically at religions' resources for transforming conflict. At the invitation of the German Federal Foreign Minister, this initiative organised a major conference in May 2017, bringing the religious factor in the spotlight of media, society, and politics. Similar initiatives exist in Finland, the Netherlands, Austria, and Switzerland. The United States founded the Office of Religion and Global Affairs at the State Department in 2013. Unfortunately, this office was significantly reduced under the Trump administration. Similar to the German task forces, this office aims to facilitate dialogue with and between religions in order to tap their constructive resources for current challenges.

I am highlighting the German and the US American initiatives in particular because they are examples for a different way of looking at religion. Oftentimes, the religious question is framed in terms of rights, for instance, when religious minorities are being discriminated against and persecuted. While the issue of religious freedom is certainly of major importance, it frames the discussion in a certain way, especially if it is the dominant lens through which religion is viewed. Not only can rights-talk serve to alienate non-Western conversation partners who in the worst case might perceive it as a Trojan horse for Western neo-colonial ambitions, it also serves to associate "religion" primarily with "problem". Instead, these initiatives look at the significant impact of religion for positive and constructive social change. Religious engagement thus comes to the forefront. With religious communities constituting the largest civil society institutions worldwide, their impact on public and global issues can hardly be overestimated. This was exactly the rationale behind the high-profile conference on religions' contributions to peace initiated by the German Foreign Ministry in 2017. Yet there are many more issues on the table. Next to peace and conflict, there are hunger and poverty, migration, and climate change, to name just a few. To explore and analyse the role of religion in these different challenges, as summarised by the SDGs, is part of the objective of this volume.

Wanted: Religious Literacy

Given the impact of religion – for good or bad – on numerous issues of our modern lives, what is needed is competence in deciphering and understanding religion and its roles in the making of modern societies. Diane L. Moore (2016: 27) from Harvard's Religious Literacy Project argues, "Understanding these complex religious influences is a critical dimension of understanding modern human affairs across the full spectrum of endeavours in local, national and global arenas. An important dimension of diminishing religious illiteracy is to provide resources for how to recognise, understand, and analyse religious influences in contemporary life". Western thinking has for so long been dominated by the assumption of a post-religious world that religious literacy has continued to decline. Religion in the public sphere – be it politics, education, or media – often evokes uneasiness coupled with helplessness. Religion is deemed too complex on the one hand and too problematic on the other hand, both resulting in ignorance and neglect. This has disastrous consequences. If religion and its influences on individual and social processes are not adequately understood, prejudices and misunderstandings abound, leading ultimately to hostility, discrimination, and violence. At the same time, religious literacy helps in reducing stereotypes and prejudices by building mutual understanding, tolerance, and trust. Recognising the importance of religious literacy in different dimensions of global diplomacy and security-building, the Organisation for Security and Co-operation (OSCE) Network not only advocates for the involvement of religious leaders and congregations in joint efforts, but explicitly calls for investment in religious literacy, particularly among policymakers, senior management in the public and private sectors, and in the media. Concretely, the OSCE Network suggests developing modules on religious literacy destined for tertiary education. "Introducing such modules could contribute over time to conflict prevention, the building of a culture of mutual acceptance, and societal development" (McDonagh 2019: 12).

Other initiatives, such as the United Kingdom based Religion Media Centre (RMC), do not promote religion in the media but, instead, assist the media in providing helpful and accurate information based on their motto: "religion matters – it deserves to be covered fairly and accurately" (RMC 2022: n.p.). Projects such as these aim to increase religious literacy through the provision of theoretical and practical training in the fields of education, media, government, humanitarian action, journalism, and activism.

2
THE SUSTAINABLE DEVELOPMENT GOALS AND RELIGION – THE RISE OF FAITH ACTORS IN DEVELOPMENT

A New Framework for a Better World: The 17 SDGs

In 2015 when almost all of the world's nations adopted the 2030 Agenda for Sustainable Development with 17 SDGs at its core, the largest civil society consultation ever had come to a remarkable conclusion. In several important ways the SDGs differ from their predecessors, the Millennium Development Goals (MDGs). In 2000, the MDGs were agreed upon by the UN with hardly any involvement from civil society. In contrast, the process leading to the SDGs included the call to each and every global citizen to make his/her voice heard via the website www.worldwewant2015.org. The diversity of the process is mirrored by the results, when 17 SDGs subdivided into 169 targets succeeded the eight MDGs. The different SDGs are united by the acknowledgement that the MDGs' goal to halve extreme poverty by 2015 can only be achieved if it is seen as interrelated with various other strategies, including those for improving health and education; strengthening peace and justice; and caring for our climate, forests, and oceans. While the MDGs were oftentimes perceived as a one-sided agenda from the Global North targeting the Global South, the SDGs apply to the entire globe. And yet another distinctive feature of the SDGs is their acknowledgement of the importance of local ownership. Local ownership can be achieved only if local actors and communities are being involved. In many countries, these include faith communities and religious actors.

The process leading up to the SDGs began many years earlier. Milestones include the Earth Summit in Rio de Janeiro, Brazil, in 1992, when most of the world's countries adopted the Agenda 21. This agenda included a comprehensive plan of action for sustainable development, with a focus on both humans and the environment. In 2000, these countries adopted the Millennium Declaration with eight MDGs at its core, aiming to reduce extreme poverty by 50% by the target

DOI: 10.4324/9781003332275-4

date of 2015 (UN: n.d.). Two years later, at the World Summit on Sustainable Development in Johannesburg, South Africa, the importance of multilateral partnerships was affirmed in the Johannesburg Declaration on Sustainable Development and the Plan of Implementation. In June 2012, two decades after hosting the Earth Summit, Rio de Janeiro again made history. At the UN Conference on Sustainable Development (Rio +20), participating nations adopted the document "The Future We Want", thereby starting a process in order to move beyond the MDGs and to establish a set of successors, the SDGs. The UN High-level Political Forum on Sustainable Development (HLPF) was created. The same year (2012) saw the creation of the Joint Learning Initiative on Faith & Local Communities (JLI). This initiative brings together academics, policymakers, and practitioners in an international collaboration for strengthening evidence-based faith engagement for achieving humanitarian development goals. In 2013, the UN General Assembly established the Open Working Group, a 30-member committee tasked with developing a proposal on the SDGs, accompanied by an unprecedented effort to include civil society. From these discussions, the 2030 Agenda for Sustainable Development with its 17 SDGs emerged, to be adopted at the UN Sustainable Development Summit in September 2015. With its threefold understanding of development as sustainable economic, social, and environmental development, the 2030 Agenda for Sustainable Development had explicitly moved beyond the former one-sided and deficient development concept that focused primarily on economic growth.

Today, the Secretariat for the SDGs is provided by the Division for Sustainable Development Goals (DSDG) within the UN Department of Economic and Social Affairs (UNDESA). The DSDG leads both the evaluation of the implementation of the 2030 Agenda within the UN system and advocacy and outreach activities relating to the SDGs. The DSDG further provides support and capacity-building to themes related to the SDGs such as water, energy, transport, partnerships, the Global Sustainable Development Report (GSDR), and Small Island Developing States. Yet for the 2030 Agenda to become a reality and for the SDGs to become more than mere goals, all relevant actors and stakeholders are called upon to identify with and help implement the SDGs. This brings us back to the role of religious actors and communities in development.

Rediscovering Religion in Development

The rediscovery of religion in the West – after decades of sidelining the religious factor – is clearly visible also in development studies, policy, and practice. For the past decade or so, the role of faith actors in development has been attracting increasing attention (Rakodi 2015). One indication of the newfound interest in religion is the fact that greater parts of development aid are now being distributed to recipient countries via the channels of FBOs (Tomalin et al. 2019: 102). Yet religion has never been truly absent in development. Quite on the contrary. In colonial times, for example, religion was a constant companion in many colonial contexts. Colonial powers included missionaries, who introduced their brand of religion, mostly Christianity, to the local people. While there are countless experiences of gross injustice and violence done in the name of a Christian God, many missionaries also had a development agenda in the sense that they viewed it as their Christian duty to educate, heal the sick, and alleviate poverty. Schools, hospitals, and orphanages were built. According to the United Nations International Children's Emergency Fund (UNICEF), religions still provide or support 50% of all schools, and 64% of schools in sub-Saharan Africa. Well aware of the ambiguous outcomes of missionary efforts, South Africa's first black president Nelson Mandela declared, "My generation is the product of missionary education. Without [that] I would not be here today. I will never have sufficient words to thank the missionaries for what they did for us" (Mandela 1998, quoted in Gifford 2016: 85).

This early link between religion and development became all but forgotten in the years after World War II. In the West, secularism was on the rise, strengthened by the post-Enlightenment paradigm that conceived of religion as a strictly private matter with no relevance in the public sphere. This brand of secularism was not only descriptive in that it aimed to represent existing realities, but it was also normative, claiming that religion ought not to have a say in public issues, including development. Yet this view not only ignored the religious roots of Western development, but misrepresented real-life circumstances. Far from becoming extinct, religion around the world continued to influence how people and communities functioned, thought and acted. For the religious factor to be eventually rediscovered in development, several factors played together. For one, the empirical grounds for the secularisation thesis became increasingly shaky. Contrary to its prediction of an ever more secular age, religion did not retreat, but most faith traditions actually increased in membership – with the notable geographical exception of Europe (cf. Chapter 1). Then, a lopsided, predominately economically driven development agenda in the 1980s ultimately led to what became known as the "lost decade" for development. The World Bank Development Report of 1990 had to admit that poverty alleviation and basic needs provision had turned out to be a "disaster indeed" (World Bank 1990: 7). For sub-Saharan Africa, for example, the focus on structural change and liberalisation had led to a disastrous decade, supporting the realisation that development needs a more holistic approach inclusive of religious values and faith perspectives. In addition, the turn to religion in development was facilitated by the rise of a new category of civil society engagement, the non-governmental organisation (NGO). This in turn led to the emergence of a specific category of religiously based NGOs, the so-called faith-based organisations (FBOs). Since their impact on development practice up to this day can hardly be overestimated, this development warrants a closer look. First, however, we need to clarify what exactly we are talking about.

Meet the (Not So) New Players in Development: Faith Actors and FBOs

NGOs, FBOs, RNGOs, INGOs. International development has no shortage on acronyms. The confusion this can cause is not exactly alleviated by the fact that some entities do not have a clear-cut definition. While an international NGO (INGO) specifies the concept of an NGO in terms of internationality, the term FBO refers to the same entities as religious NGOs (RNGOs), yet is more frequently employed. The vast diversity within the FBO landscape regarding religious affiliation, scope, organisational and normative structure, finances, etc., contributes to the challenges of arriving at a clear definition. As a working definition of FBOs, I employ Julia Berger's (2003: 1) proposal, who defines FBOs as "formal organizations whose identity and mission are self-consciously derived from the teachings of one or more religious or spiritual traditions and which operate on a non-profit, independent, voluntary basis to promote and realize collectively articulated ideas about the public good at the national or international level".

Berger's definition points to two aspects that are crucial for a closer analysis of FBOs, namely faith and praxis. While one FBO is sure to differ from the next in many respects, their shared DNA is the linkage of a faith component with a praxis component. Based on this common structural characteristic, Ron Sider and Heidi Unruh (2004) mapped out six different types of FBOs active in development. FBOs may be engaged in (1) faith-permeated development work by explicitly expressing the faith component; (2) faith-centred development work through a strong, yet somewhat implicit reference to faith; (3) faith-affiliated development work with the faith component being present on the level of experience and/or structure; (4) development work with a faith-background, displaying a loose connection with faith traditions; (5) development work in faith-secular partnerships that exemplify tolerance of different worldviews; and (6) development work as a quasi-secular organisation in which FBOs do not reveal any notable connection with a religious tradition. This sixth category – which seems to fit many of the large, formal, and international FBOs such as World Vision – needs a bit more differentiation. Rather than becoming quasi-secular organisations, FBOs have often learnt the art of translation. While they converse with their religious base, often their donors, by using religious language, they translate their religious concepts into secular language when engaging with secular development players such as the UN. While the strength of this typology lies in that it helps to structure and analyse different kinds of FBOs based on the relationship between their faith and praxis components, it should not be misunderstood as a fixed scheme. Rather, FBOs are as dynamic as they are diverse, able to shift emphases and renegotiate their specific view of relating faith and praxis over time, not least by way of adapting to new situations and contexts. While the concept of FBOs is useful in that it captures the specificity, namely the faith component, of one particular group of actors in development, it does not capture the whole range of actors involved. This is why the term "faith actors" has been introduced recently as the overarching concept (Tomalin et al. 2019: 105), which includes, yet is not limited to FBOs.

The Rise of Faith Actors and FBOs in Global Development – Prelude (1950s to 2000)

The following presents a rough overview of major hallmarks in the relationship between FBOs and development, without any claims to comprehensiveness (for a helpful overview cf. also JLI 2022: 13–20). In the continuing rise of FBOs and faith actors, we can roughly distinguish between two phases (cf. Koehrsen & Heuser 2020) with the year 2000 as the turning point. The era pre-2000 is largely one of "avoiding/ignoring religions in development" (JLI 2022: 13). As a specific brand of NGO, the development of FBOs dates back to the post-World War II era and, more specifically, to the end of the Cold War. The new historical context gave way to the emergence of civil society as the "third sector", next to the systems of state politics and economics. When the term NGO was coined in the 1950s, it also encompassed FBOs, such as in that era established organisations like World Vision, CAFOD, and Bread for the World. Expanding in the 1960s, FBOs – mostly with Christian roots – started to become more publicly visible in the 1970s as they voiced criticism on development policies by the state. FBO-led alternative approaches in development attracted increasing attention, while FBOs started to find their own distinct voices in related areas as well, such as conflict transformation and peace, environment, and justice.

"The breakthrough of FBOs in global arenas of development happened from the 1980s and particularly in the 1990s" (Koehrsen & Heuser 2020: 4), not least prompted by the deep-set crisis in development theory and praxis. The standard paradigm of a linear understanding of development as continuing economic growth had proven not only to be not helpful, but in fact detrimental to developmental endeavours. The realisation of the "lost decade" in development was accompanied by a general sense of disillusionment with economic progress as the Club of Rome report of 1972 had raised awareness of the "Limits to Growth". A paradigm change seemed inevitable.

In the 1980s, the concept of sustainability was introduced to development. Here, the 1987 report "Our Common Future" by the World Commission on Environment and Development (WCED) (also known as the Brundtland Commission) became influential. Sustainability was defined as meeting "the needs of the present without compromising the ability of future generations to meet their own needs" (WCED 1987: §27). The Brundtland Commission also pointed to the need for "effective citizen participation in decision making" (WCED1987: §28). The role of civil society, of grassroots-movements, and of bottom-up initiatives came into view as much needed supplements to government-led top-down approaches. The Brundtland Commission thereby became instrumental in the formal inclusion of NGOs and FBOs into the global development arena. With these (not so) new players, often from a Christian background, alternative and holistic notions of development came into view, including "softer" factors such as trust, holistic well-being, and empowerment.

The Rise of Faith Actors and FBOs in Global Development – Towards Inclusion (2000 to the Present)

The second phase is marked by the paradigm shift connected to the MDGs in the year 2000. With identifying eight goals to be reached until 2015, poverty alleviation became the central focus of the MDGs. For many faith actors, the MDGs touched upon core parts of their teaching, including love of the neighbour and solidarity with the poor and marginalised. They therefore not only identified with much of the MDG agenda, but also looked for ways to engage constructively with these goals. One prominent example is the Jubilee 2000 campaign. Drawing on the biblical concept of jubilee – calling for the release of debt for the poor at certain times – different Christian initiatives, mostly affiliated with mainline churches, created an international and interdenominational network in 1997. The goal of this coalition was to lobby for a relief of the so-called odious debts of developing countries and for the establishment of fair and transparent arbitration procedures. Supported by influential faith actors such as Pope John Paul II and the World Council of Churches (WCC), the Jubilee 2000 campaign united numerous advocates worldwide. Their engagement bore fruits. In 1999, the G8 Cologne Summit adopted the HIPC (Heavily Indebted Poor Countries)-Initiative. According to the HIPC-Initiative, about USD 70 billion of odious debts of 35 of the poorest countries were cancelled. Due to their debt relief, these countries were then enabled to employ their resources for developmental purposes, rather than having to use it to pay back donor countries. The Jubilee campaign was remarkable not only because of the broad alliance between different FBOs, its global reach, and, not least, its success, but also because it brought a new dimension of FBO engagement to the forefront, namely advocacy (cf. Freeman 2020). The traditional Christian understanding of being church through proclaiming the good news and serving the needy was now being supplemented by an advocacy focus. Lobbying in local, national, and global contexts led in turn to an increased visibility of FBOs in the development arena. Governments and non-faith-based NGOs started paying attention to FBOs and slowly recognised them as social actors in their own right.

The year 2000 saw yet another important initiative that helped to further include FBOs in the development arena (for a helpful overview of global initiatives cf. Tomalin et al. 2019: 104). The World Faiths Development Dialogue (WFDD) brought together actors from development, FBOs, and academics. The dialogue was initiated by former World Bank president James Wolfensohn and the then Archbishop of Canterbury, Lord Carey of Clifton. For some years, the World Bank's (now defunct) unit Development Dialogue on Values and Ethics (DDVE) became a leading player in this field (cf. Marshall & Van Saanen 2007). At the same time, the UK initiated a government funded programme to further explore the role of religion in development, the Religions and Development (RaD) Research Programme that worked from 2005 to 2010. And on the level of the UN, the UN Interagency Task Force (UNIATF) on Religion and Development was initiated in

2007, notably publishing "Guidelines for Engaging Faith-Based Organizations as Cultural Agents of Change" in 2009.

The UNIATF, now known as the UN Interagency Task Force on Engaging Religion and Sustainable Development (UN IATF-R), became instrumental in engaging religious actors in the process that led to the SDGs and signalled a second phase in the rise of FBOs. In 2014, the World Bank Faith Initiative was established. By means of this initiative, the World Bank Group sought to revitalise "its engagement with faith-based and religious organizations. They did so based on a recognition that faith-based and religious organizations are often doing the essential work on the frontlines of combating extreme poverty, protecting the vulnerable, delivering essential services, and alleviating suffering" (Evans 2020: 28). In 2015, the World Bank spearheaded "Ending Extreme Poverty: A Moral and Spiritual Imperative". One of the results of this new initiative was the high-profile conference in June 2015, "Religion & Sustainable Development: Building Partnerships to End Extreme Poverty". The focus on partnerships with and between religious actors was mirrored also in a conference hosted by the German government in Berlin in 2016, "Partners for Change – Religions and the 2030 Agenda". This conference resulted in the establishment of the International Partnership on Religion and Sustainable Development (PaRD) that

> ... brings together governmental and intergovernmental entities with diverse civil society organisations (CSOs) and faith-based organisations (FBOs), to engage the social capital and capacities vested in diverse faith communities for sustainable development and humanitarian assistance in the spirit of the 2030 Agenda for Sustainable Development.
>
> *(PaRD n.d.: para 1)*

This very broad overview closes midstream, so to speak, with the "Evidence Summit on Strategic Religious Engagement" of 2020, sponsored and hosted by the US Agency for International Development (USAID), bringing together leading experts to "review and discuss existing evidence about, and experience in, partnering with local religious communities and faith-based organizations in relief and development, as well as the implications for policy and practice" (Seiple et al. 2021: 2) (for a very helpful survey of the field in general and the Summit in particular cf. Marshall et al. 2021). To sum up, the past years have seen major shifts in development studies, policy, and practice. Having been more or less overlooked before, faith actors have been slowly accepted and at times even embraced by non-faith development agencies. Yet while the overview above shows increasing formal inclusion of religion in national and international development fields, what does this look like on the more local and regional levels?

Studying the engagement of faith actors with the SDGs, a major research project led by Jörg Haustein and Emma Tomalin explored the participation of faith actors in the consultation process to set up the SDGs (Haustein & Tomalin 2019; Tomalin et al. 2019). Their study included conducting workshops with various faith actors in Birmingham, New Delhi, and Addis Ababa. Despite the differences in terms of contexts and faith actors involved, the results were quite similar and rather sobering. Participants of the Birmingham workshop, mostly representatives of large international FBOs, "did not feel that there had been a particular effort by the UN to consult FBOs or other faith actors about the SDGs" (Tomalin et al. 2019: 110). FBOs that were involved were seen to be engaged rather as NGOs, with their faith component being incidental. Most of the workshop participants in New Delhi, again mostly affiliated with larger international FBOs or apex bodies, "were unaware that the consultations were going on" (Tomalin et al. 2019: 110). A similar picture presented itself in Addis Ababa, where "none of the assembled organizations had participated in any kind of national or international consultation about the SDGs, with the exception of one academic" (Tomalin et al. 2019: 110). Without overstretching the results of this one study, it seems safe to say that a lot remains to be done to ensure the participation of faith actors on the ground in global development discourse, policy, and practice. "Global development institutions are still, on the whole, dominated by secularist approaches and considerations of religion, and the contribution of faith actors are still a long way off being 'mainstreamed'" (Tomalin et al. 2019: 107).

With this overview of the developments that have led to the increasing inclusion of FBOs as relevant actors in development theory and practice in mind, we turn now to the exploration of the specific contributions of FBOs in the context of development and poverty alleviation, including their respective strengths and weaknesses as compared to non-FBOs.

3
MEET THE FAMILY – RELIGION'S DIFFERENT FACES IN DEVELOPMENT

One Name, Many Faces

Religion comes in many different forms and shapes. While this includes different religions such as Islam or African Traditional Religion (ATR), the focus here is on different ways religion manifests itself. In order to better grasp the sometimes nebulous "religious factor", scholar-practitioners Richard Friedli, Owen Frazer, and Mark Owen distinguish between six different ways of thinking about religion (Frazer & Friedli 2015; Frazer & Owen 2018) to which I will add one additional dimension at the beginning. While their specific focus is on better understanding the role of religion in conflict, their insights can be made fruitful for the larger context of development. This in turn will help us to better understand the specific potentials and problems of faith actors in development discussed in Chapter 6 (cf. also Schliesser et al. 2021: 28–36). Each manifestation of religion will be briefly introduced, followed by a set of questions. These questions can be helpful for analysing the role of religion in a certain context and when working with faith actors in development. And again, the ambivalence of religion shines through its different faces. While the strength of the following multidimensional model lies in that it highlights specific aspects and therefore reduces blind spots in the analysis of religion in development, it must not be misunderstood as a fixed scheme. For the boundaries between these dimensions remain fluid and overlaps can occur frequently. The aim of this model is to make the analysis of religion in a certain context as differentiated as necessary and as simple as possible.

Religion as Religio-Scape: Demographics, Dynamics, and Trends

It is helpful to precede Frazer, Friedli, and Owen's six dimensions by a demographic perspective. Before analysing the different functions, shapes, and roles of

DOI: 10.4324/9781003332275-5

religion in a certain context, it is necessary to gain an overview of the religio-scape on micro, meso, and meta levels. Here, it is of interest to look at the dominant faith traditions in a particular context as well as at current trends and dynamics. Syria, for instance, has traditionally been a multireligious country. In 2000, a majority of about 74% were Sunnites, 11% Alawites, 7% Christians, and 3% Druze (Encyclopaedia Britannica 2000) with Shiites, Yasidi, and Jews also present. Due to ISIS and civil war, the religio-scape has been shifting as religious minorities became targets of ethnic and religious cleansing. Developmental efforts after the war will need to take these new realities into account. For the analysis of religion in a certain context of development, questions to ask include: How is the religio-scape composed? What are long-term and current trends? If religious demographics are shifting, what are the underlying reasons?

Religion as Community: Relationships and Identities

French sociologist Émile Durkheim (1915: 47) famously describes the community aspect of religion in terms of "one single moral community called a Church", uniting all those who adhere to "a unified system of beliefs and practices relative to sacred things". In this way, religion functions to help establish societal structures and institutions. This includes the legitimation of authority and certain roles, for instance, the roles of men and women. With the creation of community comes the building of relationships as people connect on the basis of religion, at times even beyond the borders of ethnicity and nationality. As relational beings, our identities and self-understandings are significantly formed by means of relationships. While the relationship and identity forming aspect of religion can function in an inclusive, boundary transcending way, it can also work the opposite way, when an "us" is established against a "them". This "Othering" then creates divisive boundaries rather than inclusion. Many current brands of religio-nationalist identity formation, such as Hindu nationalism in India, or Buddhist nationalism in Sri Lanka, work on the basis of this exclusionist feature of religion. Questions to ask here include: How does religion serve to include and exclude people? How can the capacity for relationship building of faith actors help to connect people on the topic of sustainable development?

Religion as Teachings: Concepts, Norms, and Values

With Durkheim and the "functionalist" school focusing on the functions of religion, the "substantial" perspective looks at the content of a religion, i.e. its teachings and doctrines. Religious teachings, for instance, in the form of Holy Scriptures like the Torah, Bible, or Qur'an, are of central importance in many religions. Religious teachings contain the basis for what to believe (dogmatics) and how to live accordingly (ethics). Oftentimes, they include specific concepts (such as the belief in an afterlife), norms (for example, "Thou shalt not kill"), and values (such as the importance of compassion or love). Depending on the degree of individual and collective commitment, these teachings can exercise major influence on how people think and act. Again, the ambiguous nature of religion becomes apparent when its teachings can be employed for positive ends, such as for peace and reconciliation, or in a destructive way by calling for hatred and violence. When cooperating with faith actors in the context of development, it is helpful to connect to specific religious topics such as care of creation, justice, and peace. Questions to ask for a constructive engagement of faith actors include: Which religious concepts or values can be identified that relate to topics of development? How are they being used? How can they be employed in a way that furthers dialogue and diapraxis in the context of development?

Religion as Spirituality: Personal Experience, Motivation, and Meaning

While religious teachings come with a strong cognitive dimension, spirituality focuses on religion's experiential and existential sides. Personal experience of religion can be connected to emotions, to a sense of motivation and to meaning. It can manifest itself in a certain lifestyle, individually, but also collectively such as in a religious order. As with the other manifestations of religion, spirituality can move people for good and for bad, as a sense of divine calling to a certain task can be a strong motivator. For extremist Muslim jihadists, for instance, the conviction of doing the will of God has become a justification for their action (Kruglanski et al. 2009). At the same time, a sense of vocation in development work can motivate and impart meaning even when faced with little success and frustration. Faced with daily humanitarian crises, a sister of a Christian convent in war-torn Homs, Syria, frames her motivation for her engagement in the education of refugee children in terms of her personal spirituality: "I draw my strength from my faith, my hope and my love for people" (Christian Solidarity International [CSI] 2017: n.p., translation is mine). Analysing the role of religion in a certain development context, questions to ask include: What role do individual and communal spiritual experiences play? How does spirituality affect people's motivation regarding development?

Religion as Practice: Symbols and Rituals

Just as spirituality touches upon the individual's inner core, religion as practice is turned towards the outside. In symbols and rituals, religion as practice becomes visible and tangible. Religion affects how people dress, eat, and behave. Rituals structure days, months, years, and even lifetimes, providing significant support as *rites de passage* (Van Gennep 2004). Catholic Christianity, for example, has a rite or sacrament for every major turning point in life, including baptism, confirmation, marriage, and the last rites. While providing stability during life's ups and downs, rituals shared together – be it family prayer, communal worship, or a pilgrimage such as *hajj* – build and strengthen relationships, which may have both an inclusive and exclusive character. In the context of development, religious rituals such as almsgiving or tithing can play a significant role. The Muslim ritual of fasting can help to create a sense of solidarity with those in need and hunger, while the Christian ritual of the Lord's Supper is a strong reminder of equality. Questions to ask in the context of development include: What religious practices are part of people's daily lives? Which practices are detrimental for development endeavours? How can religious practices be made fruitful for development?

Religion as Institution: Leaders, Networks, and Service Delivery

For development, religion as institution is oftentimes the most accessible dimension of religion. Religious institutions include all levels from small congregations on the ground to regional and national organisations up to extensive, international networks. One needs to be aware that collaborating with religious leaders oftentimes means working with older men. Many religious institutions, including Catholic Christianity, Jewish, and Muslim communities, systematically exclude women from leadership positions. At the same time, through the hierarchy religious leaders represent, religious institutions can become powerful agents for social change. Their networks are often extensive and they have access to human, logistical, and financial resources. Not only in cases of disaster and emergency relief, religious institutions provide essential local and cultural insights. Their intimate knowledge of the context allows them to identify what is needed most and who needs it most. Many religious institutions engage in numerous kinds of service delivery, such as education, welfare, and health, making them seemingly natural partners in development. Important questions to consider in the context of religion as institution include: In what ways are religious institutions engaged in development? What are their focal points and what are they possibly neglecting?

Religion as Framework: Language and *Weltanschauung*

Religion not only shows in certain teachings or practices, but it can also influence our entire perception of reality. Religion becomes the lens through which we view the world, i.e. our *weltanschauung*. George Lindbeck (1984: 33) has this all-encompassing dimension of religion in mind when he defines religion as "a kind of cultural and/or linguistic framework or medium that shapes the entirety of life and thought". It is when different frameworks collide that we become aware of their influence. One of the first victims of such collateral damage is language. When we are no longer able to understand each other, misunderstandings arise. In development, this becomes a significant problem when different actors presuppose diverse conceptions of "equality" or "justice" or even "development" itself. Here, the art of translation is needed, not just between different languages, but also between dissimilar underlying worldviews. When approaching religion as a framework in development, helpful questions to consider include: What are the differing worldviews behind opposing discourses? How can translations between different worldviews help to reduce tensions and facilitate genuine dialogue?

Awareness of religion's different manifestations – as religio-scape, community, teachings, spirituality, practice, institution, and framework – can thus help to better understand religion when encountering its many different faces in the multiple contexts of development. While our discussion so far has focused on the return of religion, its rise in development, and its different facets, we have not yet addressed the question of why faith actors would even want to engage in political and global challenges as outlined by the SDGs. Isn't religion directed more towards the inner, spiritual self rather than meddling in worldly affairs? To this we will now turn by highlighting one particular theological paradigm within the Christian tradition.

Why Even Engage in Development? The Perspective of Christian Public Theology

In fall 2020, Switzerland turned orange. Remote farms in the countryside, major cathedrals in inner cities, alongside smaller and bigger roads: the bright orange banners of the up-coming referendum on the Responsible Business Initiative (RBI) were sported everywhere. RBI advocated that Swiss multinational "companies will be legally obliged to incorporate respect for human rights and the environment in all their business activities" (Swiss Coalition for Corporate Justice 2020: n.p.). Swiss based firms should be made liable for abuses and violations by ensuring that victims can seek redress in Switzerland. On November 29, 2020, the referendum was turned down and RBI rejected, though barely. Weeks before the referendum, the Swiss liberal political party Jungfreisinnige filed a voting rights complaint against the churches in Switzerland for their support of RBI. According to this party, the churches had violated their political neutrality by their engagement for RBI, despite the fact that "ethical questions of faith" had not even been touched by RBI in the opinion of this party (Jungfreisinnige 2020, translation is mine). In April 2021, the Swiss Federal Supreme Court rejected the complaint on the grounds that it was unsubstantiated.

The Not-So-Easy Relationship between Church and State

Next to different legal issues involved here, this example serves to illustrate fundamental theological questions regarding the relationship between theology and public issues, between faith actors such as churches and political engagement, respectively. What is the task of the church? Is it to preach and administer the sacraments? To serve the needy? To stand up against injustice? All of the above? In answer to these questions, the Christian tradition has developed a variety of different approaches to relate the church and state. One highly influential concept, the so-called "doctrine of the two kingdoms", can be traced back to German reformer Martin Luther, who thought of the secular kingdom and the spiritual kingdom in terms of two different ways of God's reign. While God rules the world through law and sword, the church is governed by God through the gospel and love. In the centuries to come, however, what was meant as a differentiation of both spheres was turned into a separation. Eventually, both spheres lost contact with each other as the spiritual realm had no more bearing on the worldly realm. In other words, the church became muted in public. This development was enhanced by the post-Enlightenment paradigm which relegated religion to the private sphere, while the public was meant to be secular.

Dietrich Bonhoeffer and the Christian Call to Responsible Action

The results were far-reaching for Christian life and ethics. Its effects were witnessed by Dietrich Bonhoeffer, a German theologian killed by the Nazis. Among his fellow pastors and Christians, Bonhoeffer saw many who privately disagreed with Nazi ideology. Yet what they believed on Sundays had no influence on how they acted on Mondays through Saturdays. Their brand of Christian faith had been entirely stripped of practical consequences and public relevance. Central Christian concepts such as vicarious representative action for the oppressed, and active love for the neighbour, remained pious words that never took on concrete shape. Too widespread was the conviction that the church was not only to be distinguished from the state, but was meant to remain separate and refrain from "meddling" in public or political affairs. Bonhoeffer recognised that the failure of most Germans, including the churches, to stand up against the Nazi regime was not only a societal and cultural problem, but a theological one as well. He passionately fought against what he unmasked as the "Pseudo-Lutheran" separation of the religious-private and the public-secular sphere. Instead, Bonhoeffer (2010: 49) emphasises: "Christians are called to action and sympathy not through their own first-hand experiences but by the immediate experience of their brothers and sisters, for whose sake Christ suffered". His conviction that Christian faith is not merely a spiritual affair but has clear consequences on one's life and action led Bonhoeffer to participate in the preparations for a coup d'état aimed to overthrow the Nazi regime. He was caught and hung on April 9, 1945, shortly before the end of the Second World War.

What is Public Theology?

Bonhoeffer's life and thoughts have inspired many Christians and non-Christians alike around the world. In Christian theology, his approach to relate church and state has been taken up by a comparatively new phenomenon called public theology. Like Bonhoeffer, public theology rejects the confinement of faith to the private arena. Rather, public theology holds on to the relevance of theology for public issues and to the relevance of public issues for theology. Public theology is an international phenomenon and at home in many different contexts. This accounts for its many different focal points. In South Africa, for instance, public theology focuses on post-apartheid challenges such as continuing injustice, unemployment, corruption, or health care, while public theology in Germany engages with the rise of populist parties and climate change. The following five characteristics serve to better define public theology (Bedford-Strohm 2009: 53): First, public theology is engaged in questions of public relevance, especially concerning social ethics. This explicitly includes sustainable development. Second, public theology is bilingual, i.e. public theologians speak both their own theological language and a language understood in public. Third, it is interdisciplinary. Fourth, it is "glocal". This means that it combines a global perspective with a particular local context. Finally, public theology takes up public concerns into its own theological deliberations.

Public Theology and Development: The Example of the RBI

Against this background it becomes clear why the criticism of the Swiss Jungfreisinnigen party is misguided. Aside from legal concerns pointing out that their criticism does not do justice to the freedom of religion guaranteed by the Swiss Constitution, their complaint demonstrates a blatant misunderstanding of the nature of the Christian faith tradition and the church, respectively. Whoever tries to separate "spiritual" issues of worship and prayer from "worldly" concerns for justice and development has not grasped that both are intrinsically interwoven in the DNA of Christian faith. South African public theologian John de Gruchy (2007: 40) points to this interconnection when he emphasises, "good public theological praxis requires a spirituality which enables a lived experience of God, with people and with creation, fed by a longing for justice and wholeness and a resistance to all that thwarts wellbeing".

From a Christian public theology perspective, a private individual Christian life is just as self-contradictory as a private church. Rather, Christian individual and communal witness cannot be but public. Churches are always public churches. So if churches in Switzerland become aware of gross violations of human rights and the natural environment by Swiss-based multinational corporations, to expect them to remain silent is to expect them to stop being Christian. From the perspective of public theology, there is no neutrality on justice. In the same vein, it seems equally off the mark when the Jungfreisinnige argue that "ethical questions of faith" had not been touched by RBI (Jungfreisinnige 2020, translation is mine). For this, criticism betrays the same misconception as if "questions of faith", be they ethical in nature or not, could ever be separated from "questions of the world". As Bonhoeffer (2005: 59) puts it: "Just as the reality of God has entered the reality of the world in Christ, what is Christian cannot be had otherwise than in what is worldly".

The example of public theology shows one way within the Christian faith tradition of how to relate state and church, public and theological matters. At the same time, public theology is no monopoly of the Christian faith tradition, but at home in many different religions. With its conviction that theology matters for public issues and vice versa, public theology becomes a natural collaboration partner for issues of sustainable development. We need to distinguish, however, between public theology as a theological–theoretical framework and as engagement. While many faith actors of different faith traditions are already engaged in public issues, it is helpful for them – and others – to situate themselves in a theological framework that interprets and supports their actions. Such a framework provides the theoretical underpinning for one's practical engagement by demonstrating in a coherent way how one's actions emerge from one's theological convictions. From this perspective, development is viewed as something intrinsic to one's faith rather than a foreign, Western and/or secular concept. Being able to rely on sound theological arguments not only helps with the continuing need for self-critical analysis of one's own action (and inaction), but also in answering internal and external critics. It therefore remains an ongoing task of the Christian and of all other faith traditions to find theological resources and approaches *from within their own traditions* to engage constructively and effectively with global issues such as sustainable development.

4
WHAT'S SO SPECIAL ABOUT THEM? POTENTIALS AND PROBLEMS OF FAITH ACTORS IN DEVELOPMENT

What's the Difference?

According to a study of how faith shapes faith-based international development organisations, "The dichotomy between FBOs and secular NGOs is rather artificial and problematic" (Ware et al. 2016: 322). This statement seems apt when it is related to certain aspects such as service delivery, where there are indeed hardly any differences between faith and secular actors. This statement is less accurate, however, when we include other factors as well. These specificities are the topic of this chapter. Obviously, faith actors play a role in development. Yet what exactly is it that faith actors bring to the field? Are their contributions any different from those of non-faith actors and, if so, how are they different? When we look at the specific potentials and problems of faith actors as compared to non-faith actors in development, there are indeed quite a number of factors that seem to stand out. These characteristics can be grouped along "formal" and "material" lines, even though the borderlines can be fuzzy at times (cf. Schliesser et al. 2021: 80). These features are not independent, but are imbedded in a particular context. This is why each characteristic is related to one or several of the dimensions of religion discussed in the previous chapter (Chapter 5). And again, it is the ambivalence of religion that shines through here as well, when "trust", for example, can be used for both good and bad.

The following model should be looked at with a few cautionary words in mind, however. For one, due to the inherent diversity of faith actors, not all faith actors display all the characteristics listed below. Secondly, nor are the following characteristics, especially the formal ones, limited to faith actors exclusively. And finally, while the following model focuses on more general attributes of faith actors in development at large, there are various additional contributions of faith actors to specific SDGs, such as the importance of rituals in conflict transformation (SDG

DOI: 10.4324/9781003332275-6

16) that go unmentioned here – but will be discussed in more details in the respective chapters. We will first look at the potentials that faith actors bring to the field of development, followed by a discussion of problems associated with them.

Faith Actors in Development: Potentials

Formal Characteristics of Faith Actors

Generating Trust (Religion as Community and Practice)

According to a 2020 Afrobarometer survey in 34 African countries, it is religious leaders who enjoy the highest level of trust of all key public officials across Africa (69%). By comparison, only 52% of people trust their president, while the parliaments are trusted by 43% of the population (Howard 2020: 9). With the number of people trusting religious leaders slightly decreasing in the last few years, faith actors are, nevertheless, still by far perceived as the most trustworthy. This is remarkable indeed and can be related to the moral credibility and authority that many religious leaders enjoy in their own communities and beyond. According to a study by Bouta et al. (2005), this trust is not least due to the fact that faith actors are seen as neutral agents who do not seek personal gain or advantage. Combined with an oftentimes long-standing history of service delivery, trust and credibility are generated, both of which are key ingredients in development work.

Forming Identities (Religion as Spirituality and Community)

Beliefs, worldviews, and values are crucial for identity formation (Erikson 1968). Religious traditions provide a context in which adolescents generate a sense of meaning, structure, and their place in the world. Additionally, religion not only functions as a social context indispensable for identity development, but also offers a spiritual context in which young people can search for meaning and belonging by experiencing themselves in relationship to God and a community of believers. As developmental psychologist Pamela King (2003: 203) points out, "[E]xisting theory and research suggest that the ideologies, relationship, and spirituality embedded within religion may provide fertile ground for identity formation. ... Faith communities can serve as a spiritual anchor for youth, providing them with a strong sense of uniqueness and personal worth as well as connecting them to something beyond themselves". While identity forming processes are especially dynamic in times of adolescence, one's identity is never entirely fixed, but continues to shift and evolve. In the context of development, the identity forming dimension of religion becomes significant not least when new ways of thinking and behaving collide with traditional systems and former ways of thinking about oneself and one's community are transformed by new perspectives. Here, the "spiritual anchor" function of faith communities can become a stabilising factor in an individual's ongoing identity formation process.

Building Relationships (Religion as Community)

Connected to their ability to generate trust, faith actors often display a remarkable competence in "the building of constructive, collaborative relationships within and across ethnic and religious groups for the common good of the entire population of a region" (Appleby 2008: 127). This competence is not only helpful in building communities and forming identities, but it is also highly valuable in terms of leading processes of social change. By engaging their spiritual and moral resources, faith actors can bring different parties together, even across boundaries of nationality or ethnicity. Based on their credibility, faith actors can furthermore help to disseminate new ideas and make development concepts understandable and acceptable in a certain community and beyond.

To better understand what is different in faith actors and how it is different, it is helpful to turn to social network analysis (Granovetter 1973). Marc Granovetter differentiates between "strong-ties groups", such as traditional villages or religious communities, and "weak-ties groups", such as chat groups. While strong-ties groups offer a high degree of support for their members, their strong group coherence makes it difficult for new concepts to gain a foothold. Weak-ties groups, on the other hand, offer less reliability, yet allow for the fast dissemination of new ideas. While faith actors often come from strong ties groups themselves, their relationship building skills allow them to act as "connectors" between both kinds of groups (Gopin 2009: 79). This mechanism is exactly what is required for sustainable social change as desired by development. For a successful paradigm change to take place in a community, connectors are needed that enjoy sufficient trust and credibility within strong-ties groups in order to ensure that new ideas are not waved off from the onset, while they can also quickly reach large numbers of people. As many examples of unsuccessful development projects illustrate, it is well possible to initiate change from the outside, such as building a school for girls. Yet for parents to keep sending their girls to school, a paradigm change in mentalities and behaviour is required that is difficult to sustain without trust, acceptance, and relationship building from within.

Facilitating Personal Transformation (Religion as Practice and Spirituality)

All development work aims at the transformation of a certain way of thinking and acting. This includes the discontinuation of negative practices, such as problematic personal hygiene, and replacing them with new ways of behaving. Yet "old habits die hard", all the more when they are deeply ingrained in culture and long-standing traditions. Religion, however, comes with the remarkable ability of initiating and supporting processes of personal transformation, which can eventually lead to social change. Pointing to the example of Pentecostal churches, anthropologist Dena Freeman (2012: 3) argues that "they are exceptionally effective at bringing about personal transformation and empowerment, they provide the moral legitimacy for a set of behaviour changes that would otherwise clash with local values, and they radically reconstruct families and communities to support these new values and new behaviours". This kind of deep reaching transformation as part of religion's practice and spirituality dimensions is needed if the changes envisioned by development are to be sustainable.

Establishing Networks (Religion as Institution)

"Religious communities are, without question, the largest and best-organized civil institutions in the world today, claiming the allegiance of billions of believers and bridging the divides of race, class and nationality. They are uniquely equipped to meet the challenges of our time: resolving conflicts, caring for the sick and needy, promoting peaceful co-existence among all peoples" (World Conference on Religion and Peace, cited in Heist & Cnaan 2016: 6). In structural terms, the "uniqueness" of religious communities addressed by the World Conference on Religion and Peace can be related to the way they interlink breadth and depth. The breadth of religious networks refers to the fact that many religious communities and institutions are connected to a well-organised, sometimes extensive network on a regional, national, or even international level, providing individual communities with financial, institutional, and human resources. At the same time, religious communities are local agents who are well familiar with the specific challenges and needs on the ground. Their local knowledge and ability to reach large numbers of people can make religious communities effective partners for sustainable development – just as they can be efficiently obstructing development.

Fundraising (Religion as Institution, Practice, and Spirituality)

Connected to the discussion of religious networks is the question of funding. "Giving USA 2020" shows that charitable giving experienced solid growth in 2019, climbing to $449.64 billion in total, one of the highest years for giving on record (Giving USA Foundation 2020). Of all recipients, religion received the greatest share of all contributions with 29%, totalling to $128.17 billion. The list of America's top 20 charities included three international FBOs in 2020. Compassion International raised $993 million, Food for the Poor $900 million, and World Vision came in at $737 million (Barrett 2020). Yet where is the money coming from? While both FBOs and secular development organisations accept government funds, FBOs oftentimes strictly limit the amount of money taken from governments. Instead, many FBOs depend on private donations so as not to compromise their independence. According to Barrett (2020), for Compassion International, 89% of their total revenue came from private donors in 2020; for Food for the Poor it was 96%; and for World Vision it was 87%. In fundraising, the community, practice, and spirituality aspects of religions come together. While especially international FBOs can rely on a large network of religious communities and donors, many religions include the practices of almsgiving to the poor and tithing, i.e. giving a tenth of one's income for charitable purposes. With these established practices, FBOs have a reliable and long-term financial basis for their development engagement.

Service Delivery (Religion as Practice)

Studying the kinds of services provided by faith-based and secular organisations, Heist and Cnaan (2016: 10) conclude: "There were no significant differences". All development organisations, regardless of a faith component, provide similar kinds of services, including education, health, orphanages, microfinance, refugee services, etc. Nevertheless, despite the overall similarities, FBOs do differ from secular NGOs in the scope of services provided. "Faith-based international organizations were covering a wider range of services while secular ones tend to specialize in limited number of service areas" (Heist & Cnaan 2016: 9). At the same time, studies also point to the fact that FBOs and secular NGOs frequently collaborate in service delivery, not least due to the "increasing realization amongst NGOs and development agencies of the crucial role that FBOs can play in the delivery of programmes that have implications for the religious beliefs of target populations" (Davis et al. 2011: 38).

While a number of the formal characteristics of faith actors mentioned above can quite easily apply to non-faith actors as well – for instance, service delivery, networking, building relationships – it is a somewhat different story with faith actors' material characteristics. Here, it seems, their uniqueness takes on an even clearer contour.

Material Characteristics of Faith Actors

Norms and Values (Religion as Teachings and Practice)

At the core of most religions are claims that are dogmatic (what to believe) and ethical (how to act) in nature. Both are often closely interrelated. One of the most widely known religious normative bodies are the Ten Commandments as part of the Jewish and Christian Holy Scriptures (Deut 5:6–21). They combine confessions of faith ("I am the Lord your God, who brought you out of Egypt, out of the land of slavery", Deut 5:6) with concrete ethical injunctions (for example, "You shall not murder", Deut 5:17). Next to concrete ethical commandments, religions provide normative orientation through values and virtues. In Islam, for instance, the virtue of compassion is meant to shape the believer's everyday life and behaviour towards others. In the context of development, the normativity of religion can become a crucial factor as it can serve to support or hinder developmental endeavours. The ethical imperative "Subdue the earth" (Gen 1:28) in the Hebrew Scriptures, for example, has long been misinterpreted in the Christian tradition in terms of domination and exploitation. Only once it is understood in the sense of responsible caretaking can it become part of a constructive ethics of sustainable development.

Here, hermeneutical competence is required of faith actors in order to identify and counter problematic interpretations within their own faith tradition.

Commitment (Religion as Teachings, Practice, and Spirituality)

From the fact that normative concepts and values are tied to dogmatic claims and confessions of faith emerges a sense of commitment and obligation for the believer. As in the case of the Ten Commandments, certain ethical injunctions are endowed with divine authority. The conviction of acting in accordance with the will of God can become a strong motivational force for faith actors, resulting in remarkable commitment even in the face of highly obstructive circumstances. A recent survey among workers in different FBOs reveals that "personal faith" is a strong intrinsic motivational factor (Bassous 2015: 378). While unwavering commitment can make faith actors effective, diligent, and reliable partners in development, it may also have the opposite effect if an individual understanding of divine will is opposed to certain SDGs, for instance, gender equality.

Resilience (Religion as Teachings, Practice, and Spirituality)

Development work comes with plenty of potential for frustration and failure. Yet if one's efforts are understood as rooted in divine calling, this allows for a different perspective on success and disappointment, respectively. In this context, Marc Gopin's (2009) concept of "incrementalism" is of interest. Gopin differentiates between first-order goals and higher-order goals in development. First-order goals refer to immediate challenges, while higher-order goals point to greater transformations that can eventually lead to paradigm shifts. While development efforts are usually directed at higher-order goals, Gopin calls for a new appreciation of "positive increments of change" (PICs), i.e. first-order goals that are significant in and of themselves. "The key criterion of evaluation is that the effect of the increment is transformative, meaning that it profoundly changes the attitude and approach of at least some people … . That is all it needs to qualify as a PIC" (Gopin 2009: 68). For faith actors, these PICs assume additional meaning when they are connected to a bigger picture. "The sacralization of the PIC can be emotionally transformative and more sustainable" (Gopin 2009: 76). Understood as part of a larger purpose, sacralised PICs can thereby help to build resilience in the midst of continuing obstacles faced by development actors.

Meaning (Religion as Spirituality and Framework)

Analysing the failure of a major World Bank-funded project in Northern Uganda, anthropologist Ben Jones points to the dimension of meaning. Even though high-powered in terms of human and financial resources, the project's different initiatives displayed "mostly technical functions and represented an ideological agenda – of rights, empowerment or participation – that had little purchase. In a fundamental way the work of NGOs lacked meaning" (Jones 2012: 200). In order for meaning to emerge, however, an existential connection is required, such as a personal link or attachment. With their common spirituality, faith actors are often better equipped to connect on a deeper and more existential level to people in religious settings. Contrary to the technical and abstract language of rights, faith language can draw on resources that relate to a shared framework in terms of the common good and human flourishing. Against this religious background, the meaningfulness of certain concepts or practices of development can be relayed in a more effective way.

Holistic Development (Religion as Practice and Spirituality)

Whether made explicit or not, each concept of development comes with a certain view of human, a particular anthropology. This in turn shapes perceptions of what is deemed necessary for human life to be fulfilling. The economic model of development, for instance, views humans primarily as needing to satisfy their physical and material needs. Religions presuppose a different kind of anthropology, one that encompasses both the material and the spiritual. Many faith actors therefore view human flourishing as a holistic process as they aim at providing sustenance for the body and the soul. In development work this can play out, for instance, when in post-genocide Rwanda development projects are coupled with reconciliation initiatives. One such example is the FBO Christian Action for Reconciliation and Social Assistance (CARSA) which provides a perpetrator (genocidaire) and a survivor pair with a cow (cf. CARSA 2022). Through Cooperative Cow Raising, relationships between former enemies are built. At the same time, both also share in the practical benefits of the animal that helps to support them and their respective families (see Chapter 13).

To sum up, while certain features of faith actors such as service delivery hardly reveal any differences to secular actors, there are a variety of contributions to the field of development specific to faith actors. These include certain normative concepts and values, a particular understanding of development, and a remarkable ability to initiate and sustain processes of personal transformation. Yet next to these potentials, faith actors are frequently associated with certain problems such as proselytisation and the incompatibility of their doctrine with certain SDGs. Religious violence is a further issue often mentioned in this context. This will be discussed in more detail in Chapter 13. At the same time, there are also certain concerns voiced from within religious communities about being instrumentalised and not accepted on equal footings.

Faith Actors in Development: Problems

Proselytisation (Religion as Community and Practice)

The fear that faith actors might instrumentalise their development work for the purpose of converting people is still widespread. In her study on (secular) development practitioners' attitudes towards religion, Nora Khalaf-Elledge (2020: 1) observes "an overwhelming reluctance to engage" with religion. She traces this reluctance not least to the immediate association of religion with proselytisation. "During interviews, multiple government participants quickly dismissed religious considerations as too risky, assuming the purpose was to change people's beliefs" (Khalaf-Elledge 2020: 9). That this fear is mostly unfounded, however, is stressed by Heist and Cnaan. "Data from numerous sources suggests that most faith-based development organizations focus on service delivery rather than on proselytization" (Heist & Cnaan 2016: 12).

In any case, we ought to take a closer look at this prejudice. For the desire to transform mindsets and change attitudes and behaviour – in short: conversion – is not limited to faith actors. Rather, it is a common feature of all development agents, just as the very term "development" implies: A process, whose outcome differs in significant ways from the beginning. This transformation is not merely descriptive, but deeply normative in nature. Berger (2003: 19) emphasises that from the start, NGOs have been moral entities, challenging "the 'Wrong' in favour of the 'Right'". The fact that all development actors engage in "conversion" does not legitimise conversion per se, however. Rather, we need to look at conversion in a much more differentiated way. Certain criteria need to be met, such as transparency, non-discrimination, and non-violence. Questions to ask of any development agents, faith-based or secular, include: Is their conversion agenda hidden or is it made transparent and communicated clearly? Does non-conversion lead to discrimination, such as exclusion from certain services? And is conversion associated with any kind of overt or hidden force or even violence? Rather than attributing conversion (wrongly) to religious actors only and rather than (unsuccessfully) trying to avoid it entirely, we should look at how conversion is being practiced in concrete situations and if the criteria of transparency, non-discrimination, and non-violence are being met.

Incompatibility with Certain SDGs (Religion as Teachings, Community, and Spirituality)

Next to proselytisation, there is the worry that faith actors might resist certain SDGs on the grounds of their dogma. Some SDGs, such as gender equality (SDG 5), peace and inclusion (SDG 16), and partnership (SDG 17), might be incompatible with certain religious views. On the one hand, these concerns seem justified based on the teachings and traditions of some religions. There are indeed faith communities that have difficulties with implementing genuine gender equality. Religious communities that are still permeated by patriarchal structures include the Catholic Church and certain brands in Islam, Judaism, and Buddhism. Other groups, such as militant Islamists, actively undermine peace and partnerships by proclaiming a violent concept of jihad. At the same time, however, a closer look reveals a much more nuanced picture. In their case study with three groups of faith actors in Birmingham, New Delhi, and Addis Ababa, Tomalin et al. (2019) explored possible challenges posed to faith actors by the SDGs. While participants of the Birmingham group indeed anticipated doctrinal or ideological tensions regarding certain SDGs, "most of our workshop participants in India and Ethiopia stressed that none of the goals were too difficult to adopt and integrate" (Tomalin et al., 2019: 113; cf. Haustein & Tomalin 2019). Tomalin et al. (2019) interpret this remarkable difference in terms of different conceptions of religion. While many Western participants were focusing on religious doctrine (i.e. religion as teachings), non-Western participants oftentimes looked at the realities of lived religion in their own contexts (i.e. religion as practice and spirituality).

Non-Western workshop participants furthermore tended to understand factual challenges to certain SDGs as rooted less in religious doctrine than in culture. While religion might be used to support certain cultural norms and behaviours, the underlying foundations of these are much more complex and include cultural dimensions of tradition, heritage, stereotypes, identity, etc. What is needed, therefore, is the hermeneutic competence to disentangle religious and cultural dimensions (which, due to their mutual reinforcement, will be possible only to a certain degree) and the ability to find resources within religion itself for constructive transformation. And who would be better positioned for this difficult task than faith actors themselves with their insider knowledge of their own faith tradition and their ability to function as immanent critics? And this is precisely what some faith actors are already doing. "Some participants saw part of their role as demonstrating to communities that their religion supports equality and human rights in an attempt to reform negative attitudes that would undermine the SDGs" (Tomalin et al., 2019: 113). In order to constructively address possible tensions between development goals and religions, we therefore do not need less religion, but more of it.

Formal Contributions, Yeah; Material Contributions, Nay: Instrumentalising Faith Actors? (Religion as Teachings, Practice, Spirituality, and Networks)

Next to the concerns of secular development agents with regards to faith actors, there are also worries from the other side, such as about a possible exploitation of the specific resources of faith actors. While their networks, their social and human capital, the trust they enjoy and their local insights are tapped into, their specific understandings of holistic development and human flourishing are being set aside. In other words, the "formal" contributions of faith actors are being used, while their "material" contributions are being ignored or even suppressed. As Haustein and Tomalin (2019: 25) point out, some faith actors "feel that their resources and capacity have been instrumentalised to serve a secular development agenda, without including the level of transformation and fundamental structural reform that their teachings and values, as well as experience, indicate are really necessary in order to reduce human suffering and inequality". From the perspective of faith actors, such a practice not only takes advantage of them, but fails to address the roots of the problems. For if secular actors collaborate with faith actors in a way that reduces them to their formal contributions, yet without allowing them to bring their underlying core convictions to the field, they risk neutralising the very specificities of faith actors. In consequence, the religious factor is deprived of its transformative potential.

Faith Actors and Secular Actors: Equal Partners in Development?

While faith actors bring to development their own faith background, though in different degrees and in different shades of visibility (cf. Sider and Unruh (2004)), they all have in common that they understand themselves as precisely this, actors in development. Just as it would be inappropriate to obscure their faith component, it is equally problematic to reduce them to their religion only. Rather, faith actors view themselves as part of the global development effort and want to be treated as equals, not as curiosities. To this end, many have learnt the art of translating their religious language into secular language, especially in secular settings such as the UN. By adapting to secular language, the lingua franca of development, FBOs not only strive for better communication, but also seek to enhance their impact in a predominately secular environment. Exploring the way World Vision interacts in the UN context, Jeffrey Haynes (2020: 107) comments, "The UN's liberal-secular focus compels all actors at the UN, including World Vision and other FBOs which wish to influence debates and discussions, to adopt 'appropriate' UN-sanctioned language in their engagements with UN actors". Their explicit development agenda is furthermore of particular relevance to faith actors in minority contexts for it gives them a way of increasing their voice and visibility in sometimes hostile surroundings. The fact that Christian girls are especially vulnerable to human trafficking in India, for example, is framed by CSI, a Christian FBO, as a human rights abuse rather than a religious issue. Using the framework of development and human rights helps religious minorities to voice their criticism of the government's oppressive Hindu-nationalist policies.

To sum up, faith actors bring to development both faith and action. Both components play out in a number of characteristics that each emphasises one or both components to different degrees. Some contributions are more formal in nature and tend to be shared more easily by non-faith actors, while others are more material and more "explicitly" religious. Next to their potentials, faith actors are also associated with particular problems, making it clear that religion's role in development must not be overestimated either. Religion is no cure-all. Yet while religion's problems should not be ignored, neither should its potentials.

PART II
Religion and the SDGs

5
"IT IS NOT GOD'S WILL FOR US TO BE POOR!" RELIGION MATTERS FOR POVERTY ALLEVIATION (SDG 1 AND 2)

Poverty's Unwelcome Comeback

Halving the number of people suffering under extreme poverty and hunger by 2015 was the first target of the MDGs. And indeed, significant progress was made. By 2015, the portion of people in developing countries living on less than 1.25 USD/day was reduced from almost 50% in 1990 to 14%. From 1990 to 1992, about 25% were undernourished, compared to 13% from 2014 to 2016 (cf. The UN Millennium Development Goal Report 2015). In 2015, the first MDG was taken up by the first two SDGs. And for a while it seemed that progress in the fight against poverty was continuing. For almost 25 years, extreme poverty was steadily declining. But now, for the first time in a generation, the quest to end poverty has suffered its worst setback, according to the World Bank Group (World Bank 2020). The COVID-19 pandemic and the war in Ukraine are intensifying the negative effects of other conflicts and climate change that were already impinging on the poverty reduction progress. While the global extreme poverty rate fell to 9.2% in 2017, from 10.1% in 2015, it rose again in 2020 and with it the number of people suffering from hunger and extreme poverty. In most regions, women and children are disproportionately affected. Until now, poverty is most prevalent in rural areas, with four out of five people below the poverty line living in rural settings. The effects of conflict and climate change, however, compounded by COVID-19, are about to create "new poor" that are likely to be more urban and work in sectors most affected by lockdowns, such as the informal services and manufacturing. "New research estimates that climate change will drive 68 million to 132 million into poverty by 2030" (World Bank 2020: n.p.). The effects of climate change will be particularly visible in sub-Saharan Africa and South Asia, regions that are already home to most of the world's poor people. Urgent and collective action is imperative – collective action meaning that all relevant actors need to be involved, including faith actors.

Religion and Poverty – A Long-Standing Relationship

Religion and poverty enjoy a long-standing relationship. And it is a relationship with multiple dimensions. Giving to the poor, for example, is an integral part of many religions. In Islam, zakat, giving alms to the needy, is considered a duty for the believer and a pillar of Muslim life, while in Christianity Jesus' admonition to see himself in each poor and oppressed person has sparked a long-standing tradition of helping the poor and vulnerable. At the same time, voluntary and religiously motivated poverty characterises, for instance, many religious orders. Monks of the Buddhist Theravada tradition or the Christian Benedictine tradition vow to a life not only of chastity, but also of poverty. Throughout the centuries, religion has also demonstrated its powerful capacity both for placating people to resign to their poverty and for motivating efforts in poverty alleviation. Again, the ambiguous nature of religion comes out in full force. While all religions are connected in some way to the social and cultural phenomenon of poverty, this relationship can be both constructive and destructive. Religion can be a help and it can be a burden; it can provide the legitimisation for poverty and for its alleviation. In order to shed some light on the entangled interrelationship between religion and poverty, we will utilise the seven dimensions or "faces" of religion, namely, religion as religio-scape, community, teachings, spirituality, practice, institution, and framework (cf. Chapter 5). They can be grouped here along the three focal points of description, interpretation, and transformation.

When exploring the interrelationship of religion and poverty, we need to first look at the socio-economic and demographic levels (cf. Schweiger 2019: 2; Keister 2011). Questions to ask here include whether members of a certain religion are more affected by poverty than others and in which social and geographical regions this might be the case, and why. Here, the practice dimension of religion also comes into view. Rather than merely looking at institutional membership, the focus is on lived religion in everyday life. As with all dimensions, context sensitivity is pivotal. With religion's inherent diversity, the link between religion and poverty on the ground is inevitably locally coloured.

Next to the more descriptive outlook of the first focal point, we need to look at the interpretative dimension of the link between religion and poverty. How do poor people understand their own poverty, their lives, and the world around them within the framework of their religion? How do they make sense of their own situation and that of others? Understanding religion as teachings, spirituality, and framework is helpful here. Looking at the relationship among religion, deprivation, and subjective well-being in impoverished neighbourhoods in New Zealand, William Hoverd and Chris Sibley (2013) found that religious people who lived in poverty displayed a higher level of subjective well-being than their non-religious neighbours in comparable outer circumstances. Once income levels rise, however, this remarkable difference is no longer visible. The results of this study seem to point therefore to the impact of religion in terms of meaning-making and resilience in the face of great adversity. At the same time, however, religion's ambiguous nature may become visible, if religious teachings, for instance, are employed to numb people's drive for improvement.

The third focal point draws attention to the transformative dimension of the relationship between religion and poverty. Here, the dimensions of religion as teachings, practice, and institution come to the fore. Recent years have seen increasing interest in exploring the role of religious networks and FBOs in the alleviation of poverty both in the Global North and the Global South (Göçmen 2013; Schliesser 2014; Heist & Cnaan 2016). Numerous FBOs worldwide – from formal international networks to local congregations – are engaged in various activities and service deliveries directed at alleviating the causes and effects of poverty. The variety of faith actors involved naturally leads to varying degrees of professionalisation and efficiency. Large international FBOs such as the International Red Cross and Red Crescent Movement, for example, are able to react in a quick and coordinated manner, drawing on a vast network of 80 million people helping those that face disaster, conflict, health and social problems. In their response to the COVID-19 pandemic in Bosnia-Herzegovina, they provided tailored assistance to the vulnerable. During the two months of the state-wide lockdown from March to May 2020, the movement distributed over 23,000 food and hygiene parcels and delivered over 500 field beds and tents (International Committee of the Red Cross [ICRC] 2021). While FBOs can be highly effective in providing urgently needed help, the influence of religious groups can at the same time be ambiguous, for instance, when it serves to heighten tensions between ethnic or religious groups. This calls for the careful evaluation of possible partners in each concrete situation. "In any case, FBOs have established themselves as important actors in the field of poverty alleviation on a global scale and became important partners for NGOs and government institutions" (Schweiger 2019: 3).

"It Is Not God's Will for Us to Be Poor!" Pentecostal Churches and Poverty Alleviation

We will now look at the role of one specific religious actor in the context of poverty alleviation, namely Pentecostal churches and the so-called "Prosperity Gospel". This branch of Christianity represents "at present (not only) in Africa, ... possibly the most dynamic religious mass movement" (Heuser 2013: 155, translation is mine), with "approximately 9 million new members per year – 25,000 a day" (Freeman 2012: 11). Pentecostalism continues to grow at an astounding rate, with most of its new members stemming from the Global South. Yet what exactly is Pentecostalism? And what does the Prosperity Gospel proclaim? Pentecostalism is a highly dynamic and fluid movement, which makes it hard to define. Yet most Pentecostal churches share the following four theological characteristics (cf. Frahm-Arp 2018: 2): (1) they engage with experiences of the Holy Spirit, including prophetic gifts; (2) their members are "born again" by accepting Jesus Christ as their personal Saviour; (3) their worldview is dualistic, divided between God and Satan, health and illness, good and evil; and (4) their personal transformation includes "breaking with the past" and a new way of life, for example, ancestor veneration is no longer acceptable. The Prosperity Gospel is a worldwide theological framework based on the view that poverty is the result of sin and can be overcome by repenting and living a God-pleasing life. Moreover, it proclaims hope for the future by emphasising that prosperity is God's reward for a Christian life, especially for "sowing seed offerings" and tithing, hard work, moral conduct, and strong prayers (cf. ed. Heuser 2015).

In the following discussion, Africa serves as a reference point, not least due to the fact that it is still the world's poorest continent. The UN Human Development Index (HDI) reveals that of the 30 countries at the lower end of the index, 28 are located in Africa (cf. The United Nations Development Programme [UNDP] Human Development Report 2020). Due to the remarkable rise of Pentecostal Christianity and the Prosperity Gospel both worldwide and particularly in Africa, Nigerian theologian George O. Folarin (2007: 73) declares, "Whatever one's attitude to the gospel (and many people do not like it), it cannot be ignored". While much can be said in terms of criticism, it is not my aim here to deliver a thorough theological critique of this strand of Christianity. Rather, the focus is on the following questions: What effect do Pentecostal Christianity and the Prosperity Gospel have on sustainable and effective poverty alleviation? What is the role of Pentecostalism's core concept of individual transformation?

Religion as Teachings: Theological Interpretation of Poverty

In the past, Christian teaching on poverty was repeatedly distorted and employed for purposes of suppression and exploitation. To this effect, Jules Renquin, Belgian minister of the colonies, instructed the first Catholic missionaries upon their arrival in the Belgian Congo, "You will ... do everything so that Blacks may be afraid of becoming rich in order to deserve heaven. ... Your knowledge of the Scriptures easily will help you find passages which recommend and get people to love poverty" (quoted in Ayedze 2009: 200). Historian Kossi Ayedze from the Republic of Togo points to the disastrous consequences of this kind of religious teaching on dealing with poverty even today: "Moneymaking was regarded as morally and religiously dangerous. The notion that the rich person could only with difficulty please God thus found its way into consciences and continues to impact the lives of many Christians in Africa" (Ayedze 2009: 208). For if in a certain framework poverty is regarded as desirable, even a Christian virtue, there is little incentive to work for social change. Against this perception of poverty, the Prosperity Gospel teaches, "It is not God's will for us to be poor!" (cf. Lotasaruaki 2006). The concrete consequences of a radically changed theological perception of poverty and material goods, respectively – from snares keeping the believer out of heaven to something rightly befitting the children of God and as a means for doing good – cannot be overestimated. According to Ayedze (2009: 209), "Christian education in Africa should rethink its teachings on wealth and poverty. This would unequivocally be the starting point in our efforts to alleviate poverty among African people".

At the same time, however, there are also problematic features of religious teachings in this context. In her study on the relationship between Pentecostal theology and political engagement, South African scholar of religion Maria Frahm-Arp (2018: 12) points out, "These churches do not encourage members to become active in civic groups or political issues. For them, this would be a waste of time and could open Christians up to attacks from the devil". Rather, this brand of Pentecostal theology views prayer against the demons of corruption and poverty as most effective, thereby neglecting the structural and political causes of poverty.

Religion as Practice: Transformation of Poverty

Multiple kinds of actions and projects are put into practice that are aimed at the alleviation of poverty. For one, there is the encouragement of entrepreneurship. As Kenyan theologian Esther M. Mombo (2009: 221) points out: "Nothing is more effective in alleviating poverty than giving individuals the chance to create small businesses". For this reason, many Pentecostal churches not only provide the normative ethical concepts needed, such as diligence and responsibility, but also practical help for business endeavours, for instance, by offering basic economics seminars (Hasu 2012: 74) or facilitating business fellowships (Togarasei 2011: 346). Religious scholar Ruth Marshall draws attention to yet another area related to the normative aspects of African religiosity, the moral realm. With regard to Nigerian Pentecostals, she observes, "(Pentecostal) husbands are less likely to abuse their wives or cheat on them, and are more likely to respect them, assist in child rearing and spend less money outside the home on drinking, entertainment or other women" (Marshall 1992: 37). Furthermore, the Prosperity Gospel's emphasis on the importance of principles such as giving and sharing helps raise awareness of and empathy with the even less fortunate. Many Pentecostal churches therefore engage in social projects such as serving meals to the poor or providing care to victims of rape or AIDS (Mathole 2008). Similarly, basic development projects in education are frequently encountered, such as alphabetising classes or the establishment of (primary) schools and universities. As Heuser (2013: 167) points out, "Poverty alleviation has meanwhile become an integral part of the self-perception of the Pentecostal Movement".

Religion as Framework: Social Interpretation of Poverty

Next to working on the level of theological perception of poverty, the Prosperity Gospel also operates on the level of social perception. Rather than accepting poverty as an inevitable fate, the Prosperity Gospel's emphasis on practices such as hard work, self-discipline, and individual responsibility helps poverty to be perceived as a challenge that can be met. As Zimbabwean theologian Lovemore Togarasei (2011: 347) puts it, "The most important contribution to poverty alleviation made by the gospel of prosperity is the positive mindset it gives to believers". Its message of "Think like a winner and you will be one" (Hasu 2012: 75), of positive confession and encouragement, helps to counter the prevailing sentiment that has been described as "Afro-pessimism" (Tetzlaff 2009). Instead, a framework built on "Afro-optimism" (Togarasei 2011: 347) and "Afro-responsibility" (Tetzlaff 2009: 482f.) is created when prosperity preachers proclaim, "You have so much ability inside you! As God created so will you create; new companies, businesses, investments, franchises ... Break the fear, be bold, be strong, stand out for God and see Him do mighty things for you!" (Hasu 2012: 76f.). As a representative study among South African Pentecostal churches reveals, their members feel "less powerless, have less fear about the future and are more willing to accept social change" than a comparative group in a non-Pentecostal setting (Dickow 2012: 193).

At the same time, however, Pentecostal poverty alleviation faces various challenges regarding the efficiency and sustainability of their engagement. For one, the efforts of Pentecostal churches in the struggle for poverty alleviation tend to be locally restricted. Projects targeting primarily those either within their own congregations or within their close vicinity, fail to reach the people beyond these limits (Heuser 2013: 167). Furthermore, Pentecostal churches at times display a lack of interest in the structural causes of poverty on political or civic levels. This is especially visible in the "miracle prosperity" type of Pentecostalism that emphasises prayer, yet can also be seen in the so-called "abilities prosperity" churches. While these churches focus on encouraging people to embrace their own abilities in order to create prosperity, they shy away from partnering with external or political actors (Frahm-Arp 2018: 13). Their unwillingness to cooperate with other actors outside their churches impinges on the effectiveness of their measures as it prevents much-needed synergistic effects.

To sum up, "[T]he gospel of prosperity is contributing, and has the potential to contribute, to poverty alleviation in Africa" (Togarasei 2011: 344). On the interpretive level, prosperity Pentecostal churches are engaged in the reinterpretation of traditional theological and social concepts of poverty, countering both a theologically grounded submission to poverty and a socially transmitted resignation to its inevitability. On the transformative level, Pentecostal churches display a vast variety of projects and initiatives designed to alleviate poverty. At the same time, certain limitations become apparent, especially if Pentecostal churches focus primarily on their own church members; if they neglect the structural and political dimensions of poverty; and if they refuse to cooperate with external and political partners. A case study from Peter White will now illustrate the potentials and problems of Pentecostal poverty alleviation in South Africa.

Spotlight: A Christian Perspective on Pentecostal Poverty Alleviation in South Africa (Peter White)

Structural and Political Factors of Poverty in South Africa

Historically, South Africa was one of the first countries in Africa to receive Pentecostalism in 1908. Pentecostalism in South Africa can be grouped into Classical Pentecostalism, Neo-Pentecostal/Charismatic churches, and Neo-Prophetic churches. Classical Pentecostal churches are traditional mainline Pentecostal churches. These churches have well-structured administrative and leadership systems that promote good stewardship and accountability. Neo-Pentecostal/Charismatic churches have almost the same doctrinal positions as the Classical Pentecostal churches, but the majority of them do not have proper administration, leadership, and succession structures. They are mostly urban centred with the objective to attract professionals and youth. The Neo-Prophetic churches, which are churches which ethos, style, and emphasis, are supposedly Pentecostal, yet depart from mainstream Pentecostal traditions to syncretic Christianity. Their beliefs and practices are fused with psycho-theology rather than biblical theology (White 2022: 129). They are usually led by ministers who claim to be prophets.

Poverty in South Africa is the product of structural and political factors, and it is also self-inflicted in several ways. The structural and political effects of poverty among black South Africans came as a result of apartheid policies and injustices in society in the areas of education, health, employment, and social benefits. On the other hand, the self-afflicted poverty is a form of poverty based on one's own decision not to overcome personal challenges for a better living. This kind of poverty is more psychological in nature. According to the Living Conditions Survey 2014/15 (Statistics South Africa [StatsSA], 2017a), in 2015 there were 35.1 million adults in South Africa. When looking at the poverty headcount by sex using the upper-bound poverty line, adult males and females experienced a headcount of 46.1% and 52.0%, respectively. So approximately half of the adult population were living below the upper-bound poverty line. The South African Multidimensional Poverty Index uses four dimensions, namely education, health, living standards, and economic activity to measure poverty (StatsSA, 2017b).

Countering Poverty: Faith and Hope Gospel

African Pentecostals approach issues of poverty from the perspective of demonic influence and address them using liberation theology and the Faith and Hope Gospel. The term "Faith and Hope Gospel" is in reference to the gospel that addresses the spiritual, emotional, social, and material needs of people by using Scripture that brings hope and causes people to exercise their faith for breakthrough and transformation in their lives. The adherents of the Faith and Hope Gospel are encouraged to look beyond their circumstance and believe in God for miracles. Their followers are encouraged to have hope and exercise their faith in every situation (White & Aikins 2021). They find comfort in statements such as, "Now faith is the substance of things hoped for, the evidence of things not seen … . But without faith it is impossible to please Him, for he who comes to God must believe that He is, and that He is a rewarder of those who diligently seek Him" (Heb 11:1, 6). The concepts of "faith" and "hope" are clearly captured in the Bible, where God is portrayed as assuring believers to have hope and to trust him to perform miracles or to turn their situation around. One example is Exodus (14: 10–14), where we read of Moses speaking to the Israelites to have hope and trust God for their deliverance from the hand of the Egyptians.

South African Pentecostal churches also use the concepts of "faithful paying of tithes" and "voluntary giving" as a way to break the bondage of poverty from one's life. Members are sometimes given the opportunity to give testimony during church services on how their faithfulness to tithes and voluntary giving have served as one of the ways to break the bondage of poverty from one's life. One challenge with the early Pentecostal movement was that their praxis promoted lazy Christians rather than innovative, entrepreneurial, and hardworking Christians. There was the assumption that prayer, faith, and obedience to the Word of God were enough for a prosperous life. Contemporary Pentecostal Christians have moved from just praying and believing in God for working miracles to personal empowerment and network support.

Apart from prayer, Pentecostals lay emphasis on the promise in the Word of God in relation to every life challenge and practice faith confession. Their ministers emphasise Bible verses such as, "I pray that you may prosper in all things and be in health, just as your soul prospers" (3 Jn 1:2). Furthermore, believers are required to care about the poor. The example of Jesus feeding the 5,000 with five loaves of bread and two fish, gives us a clear picture of his compassion for the hungry and needy. Within this context, Jesus also linked the ministry of the church to the hungry and needy to the final judgement of the nations (Matt 25: 35–40). This makes it clear that the service to the needy and poor forms part of the eschatological expectations for the final judgement of Christians. In view of these biblical points, the church is required to approach ministry from a holistic perspective.

Pneuma-diaconal Approach to Poverty Alleviation

Allan Anderson's (2000: para 17) study on Pentecostals and apartheid in South Africa reveals that,

> African Pentecostal Churches of all kinds are concerned to provide for holistic needs in many different ways, especially in helping their poor members and thereby assisting in the creation of a transnational middle class in more recent years. Therefore, some churches form funeral societies, maintain bursary funds for the education of their children, and provide assistance for members in financial distress. Some churches have 'welfare committees' responsible for feeding and clothing the poor and destitute.

I call this approach in the Pentecostal context the "Pneuma-diaconal ministry of African Pentecostalism" (White 2020: 465–466). The missional assignment of the church is transforming society through the good news, followed by acts of love. This means that the church participates in the mission of God (*missio Dei*) to transform society. This approach to mission is a contribution to national development through diaconal praxis. The pneuma-diaconal ministry should also involve the prophetic role of South African Pentecostal churches by speaking out against injustices and inequality in society.

In a research project I conducted on migrant Classical Pentecostal churches in South Africa, I noticed that the 2018 annual report of the Church of Pentecost and the CACI mentions various donations they have participated in, both at the district and local church levels. Many of these donations went to orphanages and homeless people. The CACI reports that they annually organise food distribution in Sunnyside, Pretoria, dubbed "I care". This is aimed at feeding the homeless and sharing the gospel with them.

In addition, some Pentecostal churches in South Africa organise entrepreneurial and small-scale business management seminars for their members, thereby gradually transforming the lives of some of their members. These seminars and workshops are also used as platforms for networking and sharing of business ideas as well as experiences. Members of such denominations are always encouraged to pay their tithes faithfully, since in their belief, it is one of the ways to receive multiple blessings by God as well as protection for their businesses (Mal 3:10–12). Furthermore, well-to-do members of those churches are sometimes encouraged to support needy members with small start-up capitals. However, the challenge with this approach is that there is little or no supervision for such businesses which can therefore lead to the loss of capital.

In the context of my own local church (CACI), my wife and I decided to support some key people by giving them small start-up capital. Six women were selected for funding. Our intention was that if they do well with what was given to them, additional funding would be provided as a top-up, and also to support others who are in need. We engaged with them on what they planned to invest in. A woman we had supported early did well with her funding and she is currently using her business to take care of her family. Yet the other women did not make good use of the funding. Our vision for this initiative was to empower them, yet this did not happen. In our analysis we found that there was lack of continuous monitoring and guidance on their trading activities. Additionally, some of the women had very large families, which led to the business benefits going towards the feeding of their families. This, however, did not discourage us. We still do support people in diverse ways, yet we seek to provide close monitoring, guidance, and training for the beneficiaries of the funding.

6
"HOLISTIC HEALING" – RELIGION MATTERS FOR GOOD HEALTH AND WELL-BEING (SDG 3)

COVID-19 and the Global Disruption of Health Care Improvements

Health care disruptions caused by the COVID-19 pandemic could reverse decades of improvements in many health areas, warns the UN (UNDESA n.d.; cf. SDG 3). Until 2019, major health targets such as the reduction of the global maternal mortality ratio to less than 70 per 100,000 live births by 2030 were on a comparatively good track (UNDESA n.d.; cf. SDG 3). In 2017, an overall maternal death ratio of 211 had been achieved, a 38% reduction compared with the year 2000. Despite the progress, however, every day in 2017, still about 810 women died from preventable causes related to pregnancy and childbirth, with two-thirds of these deaths occurring in sub-Saharan Africa. The reduction of preventable deaths of newborns and children under five years of age, another important health indicator, was also making headway. While still a long way from the target figure of 25 deaths per 1,000 live births, numbers were decreasing steadily, from 76 deaths in 2000 to 39 in 2018. Progress towards ending epidemics of AIDS, tuberculosis (TB), or malaria, however, had slowed even before the onset of COVID-19. In the global fight against malaria, for example, impressive improvements had been achieved until 2014, yet incidence levels have remained fairly constant since then. Now the UN predicts that due to service cancellations as a result of COVID-19, malaria deaths might increase by 100% in sub-Saharan Africa. Even before the pandemic, less than half of the global population had access to essential health services. With childhood immunisation programmes interrupted in around 70 countries by the pandemic, hundreds of thousands of additional under-5 deaths may have to be expected.

DOI: 10.4324/9781003332275-9

Good Health and Well-Being: Religion Matters

Illness, suffering, and death, but also caring for and curing the sick and infirm are traditional domains of many religions. During the 4th and 5th century, Christian bishops in the Byzantine Empire founded hospitals, a trend that intensified in the early Middle Ages, when thousands of new hospitals were established in Europe to care for lepers and those with various afflictions (Davis 2019). Other religious traditions such as Buddhism also emphasise the importance of caring for the sick, inspired by Buddha's comment, "Whoever, monks, would tend to me, he should tend to the sick" (quoted in Balboni & Balboni 2019: 150). Yet just as health care extends beyond changing dressings and administering medicine, religion impacts interrelated factors as well. Education, for example, figures strongly as a social determinant of health. Studies reveal that even basic literacy skills in girls have positive effects on the health of the next generation (LeVine et al. 2012). As Susan Holman of Harvard University's Initiative on Health, Religion, and Spirituality points out, "Religion can also profoundly influence social determinants of health (including education as well as stigma and discrimination); attitudes toward gender and suffering; health policies; ethics and law; and how we understand wellness and contagion" (quoted in The President and Fellows of Harvard College 2016: n.p.; cf. Holman 2015).

While many faith traditions emphasise the need of taking care of the sick in both a narrow and wider sense, the analysis and evaluation of faith-based health providers (FBHPs) proves difficult. The World Bank estimates that "across Africa, for example, faith-based organisations provide up to 50% of health and education services, especially in poor, remote areas" (Marshall & Marsh 2003: n.p.). The vagueness of this figure already indicates the limits of its reliability. Despite the fact that "in many low-to-middle income countries ... (FBHPs) have maintained a strong presence ... FBHPs have been neglected by the worlds of research and policy for decades" (Olivier et al. 2015: 1765). There is general agreement that FBHPs play a significant role, especially in fragile health systems, yet much more research is necessary. And even though the past decade has seen increasing interest in the role of FBHPs, it has been mostly directed at Christian actors. "Non-Christian providers, non-mainstream religious groups, and non-anglophone contexts are worryingly absent from the present analyses (particularly as there seems to be a substantial growth in Muslim health care provision in some regions of Africa)" (Olivier et al. 2015: 1772).

Just as in other areas of life, religion's ambiguous nature also plays out in health care. On the one hand, the collaboration with faith actors has been very successful, for instance, in the field of creating community acceptance for vaccinations. "Islamic groups changed perceptions in communities and they accepted vaccinations for their children. Interventions for HIV/AIDS prevention and treatment by religious leaders and health services provided through various FBOs have helped to ensure that 8 million people today have access to anti retrovirals" (UNFPA 2014: 41). On the other hand, the same UNFPA report indicates problematic areas of engaging faith actors on issues relating to health and well-being, especially in the areas of sexual and reproductive health. Here, faith communities "have the potential to – and indeed have done a great deal of harm" (UNFPA 2014: 45). This may be caused through preventing access to care or delaying life-saving interventions. Yet FBHPs are often associated with other concerns as well, namely those of imperialism, colonialism, and a hidden agenda of instrumentalising health care for the purpose of making disciples.

Medical Missionaries? Empire, Religion, and Health Care Revisited

With the colonisers came the missionaries. Histories of religion and health care commonly – and all too often rightly so – blame religion, mostly its Christian brands, for imposing not only a foreign religion and culture on other people, but also a foreign rule. Cloaked in the mantle of the Good Samaritan were unbridled desires for colonial expansion and cultural domination, for instance, on the African continent. Medical mission work "was part of a program of social and moral engineering through which 'Africa' would be saved" (Vaughan 1991: 74). Recent studies, however, challenge the dominant narrative of medical missionaries as agents of imperialism and propose a more differentiated reading of the past and present. "While evangelism was the primary focus of missionaries in the pre-colonial and colonial periods, their focus has shifted over the last half of the 20th century to one of service and social justice, including greater concern for the poor and vulnerable members of society" (Johnson & Mann Wall 2014: 223f.). In their study on women, religion and maternal health care in Ghana, Lauren Johnson and Barbra Mann Wall emphasise the particular significance of religion as teaching. Taking Catholicism as their reference point, they show how revisions of Catholic Canon Law in 1936 and a new theological perspective associated with the Second Vatican Council (1962–1965) helped to not only increase the nursing scope for women, but also create a new framework for faith-based health care. A greater appreciation of other cultures along with an emphasis on solidarity with the local people, capacity building as well as interfaith cooperation became key features of Catholic health care workers like the Medical Mission Sisters in Ghana.

These theological developments were accompanied by a shift in global health care policy. While it was oftentimes the missionaries who "provided the ordinary Africans any modern medical care and treatment" (Addae 1997: 24), the realisation grew that acute and tertiary care in hospitals were being overemphasised, while community health issues and primary care had been neglected. The Alma Ata Declaration of 1978 by the World Health Organisation (WHO) and UNICEF drew international attention to the importance of community care, education, and cooperation. Here, the spiritual dimension of the FBHPs can become a helpful resource because it connects well with existing religious frameworks and religious conceptions of well-being. The interrelationship between health or well-being and religion is described by the African Religious Health Assets Programme

(ARHAP) by pointing to the Sesotho term for health, "*bophelo*", which also means "religion". "Health and religion are one ... Whichever way you look at it, both are about the fullness of life, about one reality" (Cochrane & Gunderson 2012: 69). Their understanding of "holistic healing" (Johnson & Mann Wall 2014: 228) helps FBHPs such as the Medical Mission Sisters in their training of TBAs (Traditional Birth Assistants) and indigenous healers in nutrition and primary care as it relates well to traditional Ghanaian medicine in which spirituality takes a prominent part. Tapping into existing spiritual resources, and combining them with a focus on primary care and empowerment, appears to be a potent mix in health care. "With their emphasis on capacity building, primary care, and partnerships, the Medical Mission Sisters serve as an example of Catholic missionaries whose strategies in addressing maternal care in Ghana may offer solutions to maternal mortality in the future" (Johnson & Mann Wall 2014: 229).

"Science Says: Religion is Good for Your Health"

Though rather slowly, the Global North is catching on as the influence of religion and spirituality on issues of health and well-being is being increasingly recognised not only in the Global South, but also in secularised contexts of the Global North. A recent Forbes article points out, "[S]cience says: religion is good for your health", both in terms of mental and physical health (Roberts 2019). As a team of researchers at the Mayo Clinic summarises: "Most studies have shown that religious involvement and spirituality are associated with better health outcomes, including greater longevity, coping skills, and health-related quality of life (even during terminal illness) and less anxiety, depression, and suicide" (Mueller et al. 2001: 1225; cf. Koenig et al. 2012). Yet despite the overwhelming evidence of a positive impact of religion and spirituality on our well-being, surprisingly little research has been conducted on their interrelationship. It is noteworthy that research done in the Global North predominately focuses on religion's impact on mental health – as opposed to the focus on religion and physical health care in contexts of the Global South. In Western contexts, the positive influence of religion is mostly associated with its spiritual dimension. Situations of ill health may prompt questions of meaning and coping, i.e. areas in which religion can become a potent resource.

Yet again, religion's ambivalence shows as faith can be related to positive notions of trust, hope and optimism, thereby helping to counter stress and anxiety (Koenig 2012: 4). At the same time, however, negative interpretations of one's situation, for instance, as being punished by God for one's sins may lead to an increased stress level and depression (Koenig 2012: 5). In any case, Western health care systems are not (yet) equipped to adequately deal with the faith component of health. A US national survey on physicians' opinions on engaging patients' religious and spiritual concerns found that "the majority of physicians (65%) believe that it is good practice for physicians to address patients' spiritual concerns" (Smyre et al. 2018: 897). Yet despite the inclusion of spiritual care, for example, in national palliative care guidelines, the actual provision of spiritual care is less than secured. As one study reported, in an advanced cancer setting only 6% of patients and clinicians were provided with the opportunity for prayer (Epstein-Peterson et al. 2015). So while there is growing awareness of the impact of religion and spirituality on health and well-being in Western settings, much work needs to be done in terms of discerning, acknowledging, and integrating the spiritual needs of patients into our understanding of well-being and into our health care systems.

COVID-19 Again. Religion's Responses to the Challenges of the Pandemic

As with past pandemics, religion and the current COVID-19 pandemic interact and influence each other. Especially in the beginning days of the pandemic, media reports highlighted religion's negative influence as gatherings of faith groups repeatedly became super-spreader events. An international worship meeting at Christian Open Door Church on February 18, 2020, in Mulhouse, where France borders Germany and Switzerland, resulted in the biggest cluster of COVID-19 in France, with about 2,500 confirmed cases linked to it. Worshippers unwittingly carried the virus back to their homes in Burkina Faso, Corsica, Guyana, not to mention Central European countries such as Switzerland and Germany. Other religious super spreaders included the Hasidic community in Brooklyn. By April 2020, already more than 6,000 people in Borough Park, Brooklyn, tested positive for the virus.

At the same time, faith actors are engaged in numerous ways to counter the virus, heal the sick, and help those that are affected by it in various ways. Recognising both the importance and the experience of faith communities with earlier pandemics such as Ebola and HIV/AIDS, the WHO's office for public information on the pandemic has explicitly engaged in dialogue with religious leaders. During the Ebola outbreak in Guinea and Sierra Leone in 2014, for example, health care measures by officials to quickly bury or cremate the dead in order to minimise exposure to the virus were met with distrust and resistance in the population. Together with religious leaders, however, guidelines for safe, religiously, and culturally sensitive burials could be developed that were acceptable to the population and helped to save lives (Marshall 2020). In the current pandemic, some even attribute a "key role in the fight against the virus" to faith actors such as churches in Africa (Krause 2021: n.p.), where faith communities and religious leaders are engaged in providing both physical health care through hospitals and mobile clinics and spiritual comfort to the sick and the bereaved.

Despite their major efforts and contributions, however, "it can be easy to overlook the significant role that religious leaders and groups have played in responding to pandemics before, and in providing health care overall", says Katherine Marshall (2020: n.p.), who led the World Bank's faith and ethics initiative between 2000 and 2006 and now directs the World Faiths Development Dialogue. Drawing on responses to past pandemics, she offers lessons towards a constructive engagement of faith actors that can be related to the community, teaching, practice, and institution dimensions of religion.

Religion as Community: Personal Support and Role Models

The community dimension of religion becomes central in a pandemic. When people and their health, income, family, etc., are affected, their strong ties to communities, such as their religious home congregation, become pivotal. Established and trusted relationships provide much-needed physical, emotional, and spiritual support during this crisis. At the same time, religious leaders and church authorities assume the important functions of role models, for instance, by demonstrating correct behaviour such as quarantine and social distancing. Given the trust and moral authority that many religious leaders enjoy, their model becomes all the more important. If these exemplary roles are abused and destructive behaviour is displayed, however, detrimental effects result. While most religious gatherings have switched to online formats, pastor Tony Spell of the Life Tabernacle Church in Baton Rouge, Louisiana, has been openly resisting pandemic guidelines, holding mass worship meetings against official regulations. By telling his followers, "We're anti-mask, anti-social distancing, and anti-vaccine" (Spell, quoted in Sloan 2020: n.p.), he actively undermines efforts to contain the virus.

Religion as Teachings: Making Health Information Available and Legitimate

Faith actors are indispensable for quickly disseminating information, which becomes especially important in a crisis. At the same time, they can help to make health imperatives ("wash your hands!") more plausible by embedding them in their own respective narrative contexts. This not only makes them more understandable, but also helps to underline their importance for their specific context and situation. In Tanzania, for example, both Catholic and Protestant churches urged their members to implement hygienic measures, which put them in marked opposition to the government as Tanzania's then-president John Magufuli had been ignoring and downplaying the risk of the virus for many months (Klemm 2021). And just as religious teachings can be employed to spread false information and to increase distrust and anxiety, they can also be an important platform to counter conspiracy myths and scapegoating. In this regard, the Communion of Protestant Churches in Europe (CPCE), representing about 50 million Protestants, calls on their members, "As a witness for truth and justice, the Church counters anxiety and suspicion and the spread of conspiracy theories or scapegoating" (CPCE 2021: 15).

Religion as Practice: Safe Rituals

Religious practices such as rituals become all the more important in times of crisis like the current pandemic. While they provide much-needed stability, familiarity, and comfort, they can also become a source of concern, e.g. when burials become spreader events. As with the Ebola outbreak in 2014, faith communities can have a major impact on the occurrence of infection by the way they adapt their rituals to health requirements. Pastor Kenneth Mtata, Secretary General of the Ecumenical Council of Churches in Zimbabwe, has therefore developed online courses for pastors on safe burials (Krause 2020). Jewish and Muslim burial rituals include washing the body before burial, thus raising concerns about possibly spreading the virus. Some rabbis and imams have therefore developed practices that align with their religious traditions, yet can be conducted safely, such as wearing protective equipment while washing the body and wrapping the body in plastic before burial (Marshall 2020). Worldwide, faith communities have displayed remarkable creativity to find other formats for their established practices such as moving worship and prayer meetings online.

Religion as Institution: Networks in Times of Crisis

With their large networks on the ground and their intimate knowledge of local situations, religious leaders and communities are important partners not only for identifying who needs help in a crisis, but for mobilising financial, social, and human resources for swift and practical assistance. Service delivery related to health care becomes pivotal in pandemics, for instance, in Zimbabwe, where more than 60% of rural hospitals are being run by churches. Being aware of the difficulties, especially in rural settings, Malawian medical doctor Mwai Makoka from the WCC coordinates the collection and dissemination of best practices in order to promote an exchange of ideas among different church networks (Krause 2021). Being aware of the needs of the most desperate, including refugees and orphans, faith actors are also uniquely placed to advocate and lobby for their needs with governments and development partners.

To sum up, in view of the disastrous disruption of health care progress by the COVID-19 pandemic, and given the constructive contributions of FBHPs in the pandemic and beyond, greater efforts are direly needed to map and analyse the contributions of FBHPs in order "to increase the recognition of FBOs and to establish stronger partnerships with them … as an untapped route" to achieving SDG 3 (Widmer et al. 2011: 218). A spotlight by Azza Karam, Secretary General of Religions for Peace (RfP), will serve to illustrate the specific potentials and challenges of a multi-religious effort in countering COVID-19.

Spotlight: Multi-Religious Perspectives on Responding to the COVID-19 Pandemic (Azza Karam)

Background: But Why Religion in Public Health?

All faith traditions are rooted in, and transmitted over time, through stories. In fact, the oldest storytellers are religious leaders and community elders, who are also seen, in most parts of the world – whether we speak of indigenous peoples or the Catholic Church – as repositories of wisdom, or holders of the confessions of many. The stories, rituals, and practices define the old ways, and perhaps also the ongoing ways, in which we deal with challenges, disasters, and trauma. The stories, and their tellers, often provide sources of insight and hope. Yet, building hope in the face of adversities is not only about the contents of stories, nor even the purview of the storytellers. Religious actors (whether institutions, religious leaders, or religious development and humanitarian NGOs) are also critical social service providers. One estimate notes that in the United States, Catholic charities alone seem "to account for 17% to 34% of all non-profit social-service charity" (Keating 2013: n.p.). Add to that the diverse Protestant, Islamic, Hindu, Buddhist, and Sikh, and the figure of social service providers would rise sharply. And if this is the case in a developed economy, we should be able to safely assume that in developing countries, i.e. ones with weak government service structures, and/or those embroiled in conflicts or coping with humanitarian disasters (or both), the role of religious communities in serving the needs of diverse communities would be even higher.

In a recent study critically assessing the role of FBOs in health care, the authors refer to multiple research studies to assert the importance of partnering with FBOs as critical to strengthening public health systems, given the need to secure equity of access to health care, among other needs (Kagawa et al. 2012). They also point to the fact that religious entities have a long history of serving public health. The history of Christian engagement in health care (and all social services alongside other religious entities) has colonial roots, which bears being mindful of. Not surprisingly, perhaps, Christian entities are still the largest public health service providers the world over, not only in former colonial lands. Elsewhere I have discussed aspects of this colonial legacy, which, on the positive side, also includes building social resilience through health and education services, and as part of sustaining social cohesion. In instances where religious institutions contributed to social resilience, however, religious institutions tended to work together, rather than as individual religions/institutions.

An important aspect of the intersections of religion with public health is how some religious leaders – albeit a minority thereof – can actually perpetuate harm. Among those marginalising and discriminating against HIV-positive people since the outbreak of that pandemic in the 1980s, were religious actors. Till today, there are some religious leaders who perform marriages among minors, insisting that this is protection and purity for boys, and especially for girls. Yet other religious leaders speak up publicly for female genital mutilation (FGM), insisting it is Islamic. Others either tout or turn a blind eye to racist and supremacist jargon preached and practiced in their own communities, while some institutions and leaders stand accused of perpetuating sexual abuse. Homophobic attitudes and sermons are still prevalent in many religious institutions. In contemporary COVID-19 times, certain religious leaders continue to rail against the mandated lockdowns and have actively mobilised against the related vaccinations.

Common Action for the Common Good – The Concepts and the Actions

These are but samples of the harm being done by certain leaders of faith traditions. There are many more. What is important to note here is that in these cases where harm is done in the name of, or by a leader or representative of a religion, it is rarely the norm to find a multi-religious group of leaders who would concur with or endorse such harm. Far more frequent, indeed even normalised, is to find faith leaders working together to realise the common good. Apart from being advocates for democracy and human rights, sometimes in direct opposition to specific religious institutions colluding with political parties to sanction exclusive rhetoric, multi-religious collaborators come together to provide psycho-social and physical healing for communities, attending to refugees and displaced peoples, championing the rights of women who have suffered violence in conflicts, and/or in their own homes, and organising to advocate against this in their own communities, to name but some of their initiatives carried out through their multiple pulpits. Multi-religious advocacy, services, and solidarity has been touted worldwide, for decades, by faith leaders (and even some political leaders), specifically those who recognise the value added – and the huge challenge and reward – of making and building peace together. In the past few months our world has lost two such leaders, both of whom had a history of advocating and working concretely to realise multi-religious solidarity and service, namely: Archbishop Desmond Tutu from South Africa and Thich Nhat Hahn from Vietnam. Furthermore, both of these leaders were part of a global multi-religious movement, RfP, which continues to provide support for multi-religious collaboration as a key to public health and health security, i.e. for peace.

Examples of multi-religious action abound. Religious leaders who are members of RfP in the Central African Republic, work together with a local interreligious platform which has been moving quickly and closely to mitigate tensions between Christians and Muslims (relationships have been frayed due to violent episodes in recent years), while also dispelling myths, through all forms of media, about vaccines. In Israel and Palestine, rabbis and sheikhs are coordinating joint public awareness messages that reinforce the directives of public health officials, and are monitoring together the rising rate of domestic violence and encouraging fellow clergy to address it.

"Our government needs us to tell our people about this Covid … but also we need to understand ourselves first!" (Interview with Religions for Peace Council in Mozambique, March 2022). This was the message from many members of the RfP's Interreligious Council (IRC) in Mozambique, where an estimated three million people are projected to face high levels of food insecurity across the country due to the combined effects of the conflict in the North, weather shocks, and COVID-19 mitigation measures, which have restricted economic activity. Under a project implemented by the IRC, a total of 250 leaders from a diverse range of religions participated in COVID-19 prevention training across Mozambique.

This resulted in a much-needed, far-reaching public messaging campaign, which tackled a gamut of issues from burial customs and holiday traditions to everyday social habits. Such changes had to be communicated clearly, quickly, and widely to diverse communities of people to save lives. While these 250 religious leaders are a small percentage of the country's 30 million inhabitants, the relatively personal connections between religious leaders and their communities of followers amplified their influence, making the intersectionality of religion and public health potent. Taken together, those 250 leaders had the ear of the millions of Catholics, Muslims, Christians, Anglicans, Pentecostals, Jews, and Bahá'í in every corner of the country.

In the Democratic Republic of Congo (DRC), RfP's Multi-Religious Humanitarian Fund project targeted the 11 million residents of Kinshasa province, where high poverty rates and unsanitary conditions compounded the threat of COVID-19 for many families. Many of the residents living in Kinshasa didn't have real-time access to lifesaving health updates, so raising awareness was a necessity. The IRC-DRC helped bring together Kinshasa's tight-knit communities of Catholics, Evangelists, Muslims, Kimbagusts, Bahá'í's, and Protestants, to coordinate the work of leaders and effectively educate the community about health and hygiene best practices. One of the central on-the-ground implementers, Dr Joseph Nzumbu, is a physician at the Diabetic Clinic of the Mont Amba Hospital Centre. He worked with faith leaders to select and train ten women and ten youths from participating multi-faith communities, equipping them with knowledge they could disseminate. "The impact can be seen in that all the women and youth who attended the training and were previously ignorant of the deadly consequences of this virus, were happy to learn how they could personally help stop the spread of this disease", Dr Nzumbu said of the hygiene and COVID-19 prevention training (Interview with Religions for Peace Director of Human Resources, May 2022).

"They asked many questions and some among them told me they would go and sensitize the members of their communities" (Interview with Religions for Peace Director of Human Resources, May 2022). Those 20 trainees went on to do just that. Religion and public health intersect during times of peace and crisis, placing these trainees in a critically important role. Working in conjunction with the IRC-DRC, the trainees helped educate the public via a campaign of radio broadcasts that reached an estimated 2 million residents, as well as through more in-person efforts. Additionally, for direct services, the IRC-DRC and religious leaders worked together to select 40 mothers from the local community for an aid and training programme.

The mothers who were selected were particularly vulnerable; unemployed with little or no financial support from their families; between the ages of 15 and 30 years old; and represented the country's many faiths. In the immediate, they received COVID-19 prevention training, learning proper preventative and sanitary skills, along with up-to-date health recommendations on how to mitigate the spread of COVID-19 in, for example, multi-generational households, as well as how to properly utilise food aid and hygiene supplies. Long-term support was also kept in mind and included workshops and other programmes encouraging women-led entrepreneurship, financial independence, and education on issues of gender-based violence (GBV). Trainees and religious leaders plan to continue their public advocacy into the future, leveraging their knowledge and position to educate communities in Kinshasa about COVID-19 prevention. Already ten more young mothers have joined the support programme, which now continues to include weekly workshops for business planning and budgeting.

The Multi-religious Value Added

Because religious institutions – and their leaders – rarely work on one service aspect only (e.g., mental health; hate speech; mediating a conflict; attending to victims of violence, and so on), as is the case of most secular institutions, most of them address multiple issues at the same time, and have done so for generations. This is what we in RfP refer to as a "whole of society" approach. When these diverse religious institutions then combine their efforts in any given context, it can be a tipping point for overall social cohesion. I am not speaking of this unique advantage from an abstract perspective, but rather as someone who worked in several secular global establishments for over three decades, including two decades of addressing health needs. I can clearly see the difference between those approaches, and the ones which engage multiple religious actors to address a global pandemic, building on their unique abilities to continuously serve their communities in multiple ways on all issues.

7
"LARGEST AND MOST SUCCESSFUL EDUCATION PROVIDER ... OUTSIDE OF PUBLIC EDUCATION SYSTEMS" – RELIGION MATTERS FOR QUALITY EDUCATION (SDG 4)

Education for All?

SDG 4 aims at ensuring inclusive and equitable quality education and promoting lifelong learning opportunities for all. In addition to being seen as a basic human right, education is also widely recognised as crucial for the foundations of democracy and stable, just, and thriving societies and economies. Yet even before the onset of COVID-19 led to an unprecedented shut-down of education facilities across the globe, progress towards SDG 4 was too slow. At the end of 2019, millions of children and adolescents were not able to attend school, and even those who could, did not meet the minimum proficiency standards in reading and numeracy, according to the UN (UNDESA n.d.; cf. SDG 4). The restrictions in the wake of COVID-19, including lockdowns and the closing down of education facilities from pre-kindergarten to universities, have affected more than 90% of students worldwide, with negative effects not only on their learning outcomes, but also on their behavioural and social development. While online teaching has been made available to many students, this has not been an option for at least 500 million children and youth, especially in remote areas or fragile contexts such as conflict zones, extreme poverty, or refugee camps. "The digital divide will widen existing gaps in equality with regard to education", warns the UN (UNDESA n.d.; cf. SDG 4).

While progress has been slow – even before the outbreak of COVID-19 – it was nevertheless existent. In 2018, 84% of children enrolled completed primary school, with 70% in the year 2000. At the same time, however, in 2018, still 258 million children and youth between 6 and 17 years of age were not in school. In the same year, 86% of the global population aged 15 and older were literate. Yet 773 million adults were unable to read or write in 2018, with women making up two thirds of this group. Half of the global illiterate population lives in Southern

DOI: 10.4324/9781003332275-10

Asia and one-quarter lives in sub-Saharan Africa. Until 2015, progress was made towards raising the percentage of primary school teachers with minimum pedagogical training, but has remained at an average of 85% since then – with 64% in sub-Saharan Africa and 72% in Southern Asia. Already in 2016, an international commission's report, The Learning Generation, warned: "Unless we change course now, nearly 1 billion school-aged children will still be denied basic secondary-level skills in 2030. Even in 2050, one child in three in Africa will not be able to complete basic secondary education" (Education Commission 2016: n.p.). Next to stronger efforts in financing, changing course now also involves innovative approaches and cooperation with all relevant actors, including faith actors and their long-standing experiences in the field of education. Only our joint efforts will lead us on the path to achieving "education for all" (UNESCO 2021).

Religion and Education: Close Companions Throughout History

When in the 1990s historian of education Harold Silver (1992: 97) called for the need to bring "the religious experience into the canon of education history", he drew attention to the long-standing close relationship between religion and education. For too long, the role of religion in education had been neglected. This was despite the fact that "the link between education and religious activity is very old" (Gallego & Woodberry 2008: 3), reaching back to civilisations such as the Egyptian Empire and early Chinese and Indian dynasties. In the Roman Empire, after Emperor Constantine's conversion to Christianity in the 4th century, it was Christian churches that played an increasingly important role in providing education, combined with carrying the Christian faith into the remotest corners of the Roman Empire. Yet it was only during the Reformation in the 16th century that mass education became a prominent and – thanks to the concurrent invention of letterpress printing and the resulting drop in book prices – feasible goal. From a strictly educational point of view (and the ensuing slaughter between Protestants and Catholics aside, which reached its epitome during the horrors of the 30-Year War [1618–1648]), the Reformation and the Catholic Counter-Reformation proved enormously inspirational. Just as Lutheran reformers such as Philip Melanchthon, nicknamed "praeceptor Germaniae" ("teacher of Germany"), led efforts in providing education to the masses, the Jesuits and other Catholic orders became active in educational institutions of the Counter-Reformation.

With the onset of colonial aspirations in many European countries, the horizon for educational efforts was expanded to include the colonies. "Education was an important area through which colonialism grew roots" (Roy et al. 2020: 13). What was oftentimes viewed as a "civilising mission" included religious dimensions as well. Christian missionaries became "important agents in the development of educational systems in former colonies" (Gallego & Woodberry 2008: 6). Analysing missionary education from a market perspective, Francisco Gallego and Robert Woodberry point to the competition between Protestant and Catholic missionaries as stimulating educational development and innovation. Referring to the case of Malawi in the early 1920s, they recount a controversy between colonial officials and Protestant missionaries regarding the establishment of secondary schools. It was only when the French White Fathers arrived and opened secondary schools that the Protestants reacted immediately by establishing secondary schools as well (Gallego & Woodberry 2008: 5). While the dominant perspective within scholarship links missionary educational activity primarily to imperialism (cf. Mwiria 1991), more recent contributions argue also for the need of a "dispassionate and objective assessment of colonial education" (Whitehead 2005: 447).

Since Silver's challenge to his colleagues, research on religion and education in colonial times has gained traction. Other areas, however, remain under-researched, including the role of religious women in education, such as through convent schools (cf. Raftery 2012). In 1951 in Bangladesh, for example, the Sisters of the Holy Cross founded an establishment that would later become the renowned Holy Cross Girls' High School and College. The recent public exposure of sexual and other abuses of children in different religious educational settings worldwide, and especially in Catholic contexts, has been a catalyst for much-needed transparency and analyses of past and present abuses within faith-based institutions (for a case study on abuses of children in so-called charter schools, Protestant schools in Ireland, cf. Coleman 2001). While the role of religion in education has been a blessing to some and a curse to others, one thing remains undisputed: Religion matters in education. And it continues to matter today in our global efforts of reaching SDG 4.

How Religion Matters in Global Education Today?

With earlier efforts focusing on primary education and the inclusion of girls, global education agendas have meanwhile shifted towards full educational systems, lifelong learning, and a broader concept of inclusion. Even though education is widely accepted as fundamental for development and despite the fact that religion and education are closely intertwined, the role of faith actors has largely been neglected. According to Katherine Marshall (2018: 185), "The marginal treatment of religious facets in the global discussions is striking and puzzling. ... Religious institutions play major educational roles, and religious beliefs as to educational curricula and pedagogy are pertinent for core education goals and design". Reasons for the neglect of faith actors in education include, says Marshall, a one-sided focus on public education systems, when in many contexts faith-based education institutions are viewed as private players. Furthermore, the vast diversity within and between faith-based education providers in terms of quality, approach, and size makes any systematic evaluation difficult. The resulting lack in data and knowledge impinges in turn on their acknowledgement and inclusion in development strategies, especially on a global level. Real or perceived problems in terms of methodology, for instance, an overemphasis on rote learning rather than encouraging independent and critical thinking, and in terms of content, such as promoting exclusionary ideas or even fundamentalism and radicalism, are additional concerns, particularly in view of some Islamic education providers.

In tackling these obstacles towards a better acknowledgement and inclusion of faith-based education providers, a deeper understanding of their contributions is key, in conjunction with the need for more data. Examples such as the Catholic Fe y Alegría system, which serves the poorest and least accessible communities in Latin America (cf. Magis Americas n.d.), or the Aga Khan Development Network, founded by Aga Khan, Imam of the Ismaili community, and their commitment towards best practices and highest education standards in the developing world are powerful illustrations of the effectiveness, commitment, and success of faith-based education providers in meeting the global education challenge (cf. Aga Khan Foundation 2020). For a better understanding of how religion matters in education, we will take a closer look at different dimensions of religion as they pertain to global education challenges – while keeping in mind the vast diversity within faith-based education providers.

Religion as Community: Education of Religious Personnel and Advocacy

One important dimension of faith-based education concerns the education of future religious personnel. Religious leaders such as imams, priests, or rabbis are commonly educated at theological institutions such as madrasas, seminaries, or yeshivot. Especially in pluralist societies, transparency in the education of religious leaders becomes of specific interest to the public. Lack of clarity of the content of their education may raise suspicion regarding their (in-)compatibility with existing laws and values. The practice of imams being educated in Turkey and then sent to Germany to serve congregations in Turkish, for example, has given rise to concerns about the creation of possible parallel societies where fundamentalism may thrive. To support integration and social cohesion, the education of imams has therefore been moved to Islamic theological faculties at German universities.

The community aspect of religion becomes furthermore important in the area of advocacy and leading social change. Here, religious leaders are invaluable partners for engaging communities in key social areas, including education. Just as religious leaders can use their authority and credibility to block knowledge acquisition and exacerbate tension, their cooperation can have a lasting and positive impact. For example, "[R]eligious leadership on conservation of natural resources can make an enormous difference in shaping public attitudes" (Marshall 2018: 189).

Religion as Teachings: Religious Literacy and Values

In April 2021, a call from the Theology and Religious Studies department of Chester University, UK, went out to seek national and international support in their struggle against threatened cuts to staffing. This call responded to the questions of the specificities of religious education and to why pluralistic societies would need it – or not need it. One of the major arguments here – rightly emphasised in the Chester Call – is the growing need for religious literacy. Education systems around the world, including Western European countries, the US, and China, have undergone a major change within their educational curricula towards the marginalisation or complete exclusion of religion (Prothero 2008). This has led to a worrisome decline in religious literacy. Not only do fewer and fewer people understand their own heritage, but they also lack the hermeneutical resources to understand other people's traditions. In increasingly pluralist societies, however, social cohesion depends not least on the mutual respect of each other's identities across communities. If communities lack the literacy and the resources for "reading" and understanding each other, social tensions are the inevitable result.

Next to the skills related to religious literacy, faith-based education providers are crucial for the dissemination of values, indispensable not least for the sustainability of functioning democracies. As the so-called Böckenförde dilemma, named after the German constitutional judge Ernst-Wolfgang Böckenförde, puts it, the liberal secularised state lives by prerequisites which it cannot guarantee itself (Böckenförde 1976: 60). Rather, it depends on the values and moral substance from other societal systems such as religions. A "value-neutral" state or, for that matter, "value-free education" is thus a chimaera. It is neither possible nor is it even desirable. Rather, citizens in pluralistic, democratic societies need to collectively discern which values they want to live by, such as equality, liberty, tolerance, and solidarity. And here, faith-based education providers play a seminal role. For education systems teach and live values, disseminating them into society from pre-kindergarten through adult lifelong learning. Yet just as faith-based education can be employed for teaching hatred, intolerance, and oppression, religious education systems can help lay the foundation for social cohesion and democracy, teaching respect of difference, the dignity of everyone, and peaceful conflict resolution. In Bangladesh, for instance, "apart from providing secular education as part of the larger national education systems, [Christian education providers] also focus on moral education" (Roy et al. 2020: 11), including addressing "issues of religious diversity and pluralism in the course of their teaching" (Roy et al. 2020: 13).

Religion as Spirituality: Holistic Education and Personal Transformation

According to A.C. Bhaktivedanta Swami (Srila Prabhupada), founder of the International Society for Krishna Consciousness (ISKCON), Western education systems are incomplete due to their lack of attention to spirituality (ISKCON 2021: n.p.). Many faith-based education providers therefore combine a focus on employability, i.e. training their students to be fit for the job market, with a sense of forming the entire person through enhancing their sense of spirituality, their life skills, and deepening their moral framework. ISKCON promotes a system of learning that enables students not only to attain the goal of life, namely bringing the individual to God consciousness, but also to "improve their academic and vocational potentials, apply Vedic principles to contemporary lifestyles, and make positive contributions in society" (ISKCON 2021: n.p.). In their systematic courses that target youths between 16 and 30 years of age, for example, they focus on a holistic approach that includes moral teachings and "instructions on the means of achieving fulfilment and transformation in human life" (Roy et al. 2020: 16). ISKCON thus emphasises experiential learning and overarching skills such as positive thinking, personality development, and self-management. Although criticised for their lack of gender inclusiveness in secondary education and upwards, its innovative approach that welcomes students from all religions is exemplary as it draws attention to the resources of religious traditions in promoting spiritual well-being and social cohesion.

Religion as Institution: Access and Service Delivery to the Poor and Marginalised

Religious institutions provide educational services from pre-kindergarten to university education and life-long learning in virtually all parts of the world, covering all age groups. Despite the fact that religious institutions are prominent players in the global education landscape, it is remarkable how little reliable qualitative and quantitative data is available. While there are no reliable figures for religiously run education, guesstimates of around 50% are common. Among the better-researched religious institutions are Catholic schools, the largest faith-based educational system worldwide, with about 120,000 schools and more than 1,000 colleges and universities. In 2012, around 23,5 million students attended Catholic-affiliated education institutions in Africa (eds. Grace & O'Keefe 2007), where governments usually regard them as private schools. Yet the relationship between faith-based education providers and governments is different for each context. Islamic education in Bangladesh, for example, is provided by Alia madrasas, which belong to the state education system, while Quomi madrasas are independent (Roy et al. 2020).

Not only are religious institutions significant providers of education worldwide, but they also ensure access to education even in difficult-to-reach regions, including areas of conflict, extreme poverty, or refugee situations, as the following examples illustrate. Nobel Peace Prize Laureate Denis Mukwege, gynaecologist and founder of the Panzi Hospital in Bukavu, DRC, points out that in conflict contexts like his own, much of the needed infrastructure, including schooling, are provided by FBOs and churches (Bukavu, personal communication, 6 February 2018). Providing access to quality and inclusive education opportunities for people living in marginalised and impoverished communities, or as Fe y Alegría founder Fr. José María Vélaz puts it, "where the asphalt ends" (Magis Americas n.d.: n.p.) is the goal of the Fe y Alegría educational system that has been described as "the largest and most successful education provider in Latin America and the Caribbean outside of public education systems" (Marshall 2020: 187). Ensuring education for refugees is another field of experience for faith actors as the work of the Jesuit Refugee Service illustrates.

Religion as Framework: Pluralism and Inclusion

Faith-based education systems are more or less overtly embedded in specific frameworks. Just as religious frameworks can breed narrowmindedness, exclusion and fundamentalism, they can also model a different reality, one that is characterised by pluralism, inclusion and diversity. Based on a religious worldview, the free and equal coexistence and cooperation between different religious traditions can not only be taught, but lived out by faith-based education providers, thereby positively shaping the sense and understanding of the reality of their students. This includes challenging present realities, for instance, by modelling inclusion in the face of inequality.

Faith-based education providers such as Caritas Bangladesh deliver education "to female children, children with special needs, Adibashis, and other generally excluded groups, with no distinction of caste, religion or other markers of social difference" (Roy et al. 2020: 14). Through teaching and practicing inclusion, new and positive frameworks are being created that can impact not only individuals, but also entire societal structures. A case study from Wendy Yee Mei Tien will serve to illustrate the contributions and challenges of religion in quality education from a Malaysian Buddhist perspective.

Spotlight: A Buddhist Perspective on Wisdom and Human Values in Education in Malaysia (Wendy Yee Mei Tien)

Malaysia is a multi-ethnic society rich with diverse cultures and religions. Generally, each ethnic group practices a different religion, culture, and tradition. However, due to the process of assimilation and acculturation over long periods of living together as close-knitted communities, there are many mixed marriages and conversion into different religions across the diverse ethnic groups. Hence, it is not difficult to find Malaysian Chinese or Indians (the two main minority groups in Malaysia) who practice different religions such as Islam, Christianity, Buddhism, and Hinduism. However, as enshrined in the Constitution of Malaysia, Islam is the "religion of the Federation". Hence, Malaysian Malays are automatically born into the Islamic faith. There are provisions in the Federal Constitution of Malaysia to allow a Muslim to preach the teachings of his religion among non-Muslims. A non-Muslim is also permitted to preach the teachings of his/her religion or beliefs among people or followers of other faiths, except for Muslims. The State laws and Article 11(1) of the Malaysia Federal Constitution (Kusrin et al. 2013) contain provisions to control or restrict the spread or propagation of non-Islamic religious beliefs or faiths among followers of the Islamic religion. Thus, it is a crime to persuade, influence, force or instigate a Muslim to embrace or become a member of a religion other than Islam (Kusrin et al. 2013). As such, discussion about religion can be a very sensitive topic in Malaysia.

Despite the different theology in the diverse religions, there are common universal values across all religions. These universal values include equality, tolerance, respect, compassion, and solidarity, including the famous golden rule of "Do unto others as you would have them do unto you". These universal values are commonly used as the basis for teaching "moral" education in schools in Malaysia. This approach enables Malaysians to develop a deeper understanding and respect for the different religions while adhering to the provisions stated in the Malaysia Federal Constitution.

As a Malaysian Chinese and a Buddhist, I belong to the less than 20% of the population in Malaysia. As a faculty member teaching in one of the public universities in Malaysia, where the majority of the faculties, staff and student population are Malay Muslim, I too belong to the minority group. However, this is not an obstacle for me because I was able to share many values from the Buddhist perspective which are inclusive and humanistic.

Buddhism teaches that all people are inherently Buddhas. This philosophical perspective reflects the core spirit of the Lotus Sutra (a Buddhist scripture), one founded on faith in the inherent dignity of human beings and profound confidence in people's capacity for positive transformation. As such, all human beings, regardless of social status or academic background, are worthy of respect. In addition, Nichiren Daishonin's Buddhism expounds a principle known as "the cherry, the plum, the peach, the damson" (Wahid & Ikeda 2015: 86). The cherry, plum, peach, and damson, while all bloom to the fullest with their own unique and distinct beauty, exist in harmony with one another. Similarly, all human beings are unique in their own ways; each has a different potential. When we can respect each other despite differences in ethnicity, religion, and culture, we too can coexist harmoniously with one another. Another fundamental tenet of Buddhism is that of dependent origination. All phenomena arise from mutually interdependent relationships. In other words, Buddhism teaches that nothing can exist entirely on its own in complete isolation; all things are mutually dependent upon and influence one another. This principle of dependent origination enables us to reflect on how to establish better human relations and how interdependent and interrelated all our lives are.

To illustrate how these Buddhist perspectives and principles are used as the framework to promote inclusive and humanistic education to a diverse, multi-ethnic, and multi-religion student population in my class, I would like to share a case study of two inspiring stories. Both these stories were shared by my students in the Ethnic Relations subject class – a compulsory subject for all undergraduate students. In this class, students were taught about the concepts and social theories of inter-ethnic relations. The values and principles of acknowledging the unique potential of every individual, respecting the dignity of all lives, and the tenets of dependent origination from the Buddhist perspectives were incorporated into the discussion of inter-ethnic relations. These Buddhist perspectives were used to challenge the negative stereotypes, prejudices, and discrimination each ethnic group has against others, and to challenge individual biases towards one another. The main aim of embedding these Buddhist principles and values into the classroom discussion was to create a paradigm shift in the minds of the students from living in the stereotypical societal bubbles to awakening them to our common humanity, our interdependent relations as well as the dignity and preciousness of all lives. Until and unless students are awakened to these fundamental "truths", it will be a continuous uphill battle to tackle inter-ethnic relations in a multi-ethnic society.

Students were asked to put into practice what they have learnt in class, and after eight weeks of lectures, they were asked to reflect on and share their most unforgettable experiences. The first story was narrated by a Muslim Malay boy living with a Chinese Buddhist boy as roommates in the university dormitory. Initially, when they first became roommates, they felt uneasy as they both have very different lifestyles. The Muslim Malay boy often works till late at night while the Chinese Buddhist boy often sleeps early and prefers to be the early bird. Every morning the Muslim Malay boy would wake up very early to perform his morning prayers and then go back to sleep until the late morning, just in time for his classes. This was often the routine for both the boys. However, there were few mornings where the Muslim Malay boy overslept and missed his morning prayers. When his roommate realised it, he decided to be his roommate's alarm clock. The Chinese Buddhist boy decided to wake up every morning before the Muslim morning prayer time so that he could wake up his roommate to perform his morning prayers. Although both boys were of different backgrounds, they respected each other and celebrated their diversity in a beautiful manner. The Muslim Malay boy who narrated the story related how grateful he was to his Chinese Buddhist roommate, and he realised that differences in ethnicity and religious affiliation are not a barrier to forming genuine friendships. When we truly care for one another based on our common humanity, we can surmount ethnic and religious differences and deepen our understanding and respect for one another.

The second story was also narrated by a Muslim Malay boy who came from a poor family living in a rural village. This boy is the eldest among his five siblings. His neighbour is an Indian Hindu couple with no children. At the age of 16 years old, every evening this boy would walk to a nearby mosque to perform his evening prayers. As it was a rural village, there were no streetlights along the way from the boy's house to the mosque. Every evening the boy would walk with his flashlight to and back from the mosque. Witnessing this daily evening event, and sensing the danger for the boy to walk in pitch darkness every night, the Indian Hindu neighbour decided to fetch the boy on his motorcycle at the mosque. Initially, the boy was reluctant because he did not want to cause any inconvenience to his neighbour, but his neighbour insisted. The Indian Hindu uncle even insisted that he will wait at the mosque while the boy performs his prayers and then drive him back after he finishes his prayers. Since then, it became a daily routine for the Indian Hindu uncle to transport his neighbour – the Malay

Muslim boy – to and back from the mosque. When the boy turned 19 years old, he got admission into a local university, and he left home. Unfortunately, two weeks after his admission to the university, he heard the news that his neighbour, the Indian Hindu uncle, had passed away. The boy was very sad because he could not return to pay his last respect to this uncle whom he felt deeply indebted to. The boy cried as he was narrating this experience. He realised that people inherently possess an immense capacity for goodness, compassion to care for others, and the yearning to make a positive contribution to society. If we do not judge and stereotype a person simply by their ethnicity, or the colour of their skin, or their religious affiliation, we will be able to see the profound goodness inherent in everyone. Both these stories are classical examples depicting the inherent potential goodness in every human being and the interdependency of all lives.

The great author Leo Tolstoy (2021) once wrote that religious teaching is about explaining the purpose and meaning of life. As such, it should be the basis of any education. However, this does not mean teaching the theology of the religion in the classroom but to base the foundation of education on a holistic view of humanity and a sound philosophy of life that aims to realise the true happiness of each individual as taught in Buddhism.

Through embedding the Buddhist perspective and principles in the discourse of inter-ethnic relations in this class, students were able to reflect the universal values from the faith-based framework, including the values from their respective religions. The Buddhist principles of equality, acknowledging the unique qualities of every individual, the dignity of every life, and the principle of dependent origination are fundamental to transforming the narrow stereotypical and biased perspective of individuals to one that embraces inclusiveness, compassion, respect, and understanding. "Compassion in Buddhism does not involve the forcible suppression of our natural emotions, our likes and dislikes. Rather it is to realise that even those we dislike have qualities that can contribute to our lives and can afford us opportunity to grow in our own humanity" (Ikeda 2004: 74).

Afterall, the fundamental purpose of religion is to polish and perfect our character, to enable all humanity to coexist harmoniously and happily in this world. Therefore, it is important to translate these values into pragmatic actions in our daily lives because the true worth of religion shines only in our actions. According to the Buddhist proverb: "One is the mother of ten thousand". Therefore, through the fundamental transformation in the behaviour of an individual based on practicing the universal values of religion, in this case, the Buddhist values and principles in inter-ethnic relations, it will create a ripple effect that will effect change in another individual, in the community, and eventually the entire society.

8
"YOUR WOMEN, LET THEM BE SILENT IN THE ASSEMBLIES" – RELIGION MATTERS FOR GENDER EQUALITY (SDG 5)

Still a Long Way to Go

Recent years have seen significant progress towards ending all forms of discrimination against women and girls everywhere – until the onset of COVID-19, that is. Child marriage, for example, had been on the decline in previous years, from about one in four young women to be married as a child in 2004 to one in five in 2019 (UNDESA n.d.; cf. SDG 5). The pandemic, however, threatens this progress with up to 10 million additional girls being at risk of child marriage in the next decade. For gender parity and the empowerment of women, women's equal participation in decision-making is crucial. More women are now in leadership roles, with women's representation in the political arena higher than ever before. Nevertheless, given the current rate of progress, it would still take about 40 years until total parity is reached, with women's representation in national parliament having reached 25.6%, and in local governments 36.3%, by 2021. While some progress has also been made in ending violence against women, numbers remain alarmingly high. Surveys from the period 2000–2018 indicate that one in three women have been subjected to physical and/or sexual violence at least once in their lifetime since the age of 15. Data from 95 countries and territories for 2020 reveal, for example, that 63% still lack rape laws based on the principle of consent (UNDESA n.d.; cf. SDG 5). During the COVID-19 lockdown, domestic violence rose drastically. Helena Dalli, a member of the European Commission, points out that in France reports of domestic violence increased by 30% during lockdown, while in Belgium about 70% more calls were registered with a phone helpline (Dalli 2020). Female genital mutilation (FGM) has decreased somewhat, yet there are still countries and regions in which about 90% of girls and women have undergone this harmful practice. And what is the role of religion in all of this? With its religious (and cultural) dimensions, the example of FGM is often used to

DOI: 10.4324/9781003332275-11

illustrate the link between gender equality and religion. Yet the impact of religion reaches far deeper than individual practices such as FGM. Next to concrete actions, religion influences mindsets, habits, and what is regarded as the legitimate and appropriate "role of women" in a given context.

Where Are the Women Leaders? The Pillars of Patriarchy Revisited

The litmus test of women equality, so to speak, is women's access to leadership. Most problems addressed by SDG 5 targets, including violence against women and girls, child marriage or FGM, are in a way related to the fact that in many contexts women are still not fully equal in terms of independent decision-making, authority, and leadership. Quite the contrary is the case. In many different contexts, patriarchal structures – visible or latent – persist. One example is equal pay. Even in the Western Hemisphere, where the issues surrounding women's rights and gender equality have become pretty much mainstreamed, women are still paid less for their work compared to their male counterparts. Equal Pay Day has thus become a symbolic day in order to raise awareness of the persistent gender pay gap.

Most religious traditions are not exactly known to be at the forefront of gender equality, to put it mildly. All three Abrahamic religions, for instance, display obvious difficulties with the concept of female leadership, even though there are differences within each faith tradition. While Reform Judaism embraces female rabbis, for example, this is frowned upon by Orthodox Jews. For decades, many mainline Protestant churches have been ordaining women to be pastors; Catholic or Orthodox churches, however, are still far from taking such a step. Similarly, female imams are few and far between. Oftentimes, it is an amalgam of historical, religious, and cultural factors that defines women's religious spaces.

The past few decades, however, have witnessed significant changes and challenges to established hierarchies. The following example of the US Southern Baptist Convention (SBC), a conservative Southern evangelical organisation, aptly illustrates how entrenched gender roles are recently being contested as women are protesting their traditionally assigned spaces. While the Great Awakenings of the 18th and 19th centuries provided a platform also for women's voices, the ensuing institutionalising of American evangelicalism put an end to women's public teaching to mixed audiences. Instead, women were often confined to speaking to other women and children. A literal interpretation of the Bible together with the principle of "Biblical womanhood" served the fact that women in the SBC and other conservative evangelical congregations were found in the nurseries rather than on pulpits (Maxwell 2021). These restrictions never went entirely uncontested, however, and from the 1960s onwards, women – and men – started to critically reconsider the biblical justification for their roles. In the early 1980s, "Women in Ministry, SBC", was founded, to be echoed in the larger context of American evangelicalism by "Christians for Biblical Equality". Backlash came in the form of the Council on Biblical Manhood and Womanhood (CBMW), voicing harsh critique of "the emergence of roles for men and women in church leadership that do not conform to Biblical teaching" (CBMW 1987: n.p.). This sentiment was echoed by the Baptist Faith & Message 2000 (SBC 2022), rejecting women ordination and calling for the subordination of wives to their husbands. Yet the quest for gender equality is continuing in conservative evangelicalism, fuelled not least by abuse scandals within evangelical churches and by Southern Baptist support for Donald Trump. "As a result, influential evangelical women have encouraged their audiences to reconsider their understandings of women's roles [and to] reconsider how culture and history have influenced their views" (Maxwell 2021: n.p.). Unequal power structures and hierarchies are, however, not only visible in the (lack of) female leadership, but also take many different forms. One of its most ghastly shapes is child marriage.

Childhood Lost. Faith Actors and Child Marriage

In most child marriages, a younger girl is married to an older man; although in some countries it is not uncommon for boys to marry under the age of 18. According to the NGO Girls not Brides, every year 12 million girls are in this way robbed of their rights to health, education, and control over their own lives, despite the fact that most countries have passed laws against child marriages (cf. Girls Not Brides 2022). Reasons for child marriage are varied and often complex, including poverty, religious and cultural tradition, or – in particular dire circumstances – survival. Consequences for the girls affected by child marriage are devastating as the FBO World Vision (2022) points out. Many girls are forced to drop out of school to take up domestic responsibilities and to raise children of their own. Being still children themselves, girls are not yet physically and emotionally prepared for motherhood. They and their babies have a far higher risk for complications in childbirth. Being one of its root causes, poverty is also an ongoing consequence of child marriages. Not having had the chance for adequate education themselves, child brides often perpetuate the cycle of poverty for their own children.

With the onset of COVID-19, the numbers of early and forced marriages have risen dramatically. In view of recent harrowing statistics and briefs, Sarah Thompson (2020: n.p.) from WFDD criticises that "most of the data and analysis lack a significant faith lens and few offer actionable ways for faith leaders and groups to help combat the problem". Yet especially in religious societies, faith has a significant impact on social issues like gender equality, for good or for bad, but it is rarely ever passive. In view of Bangladesh, a predominately Muslim country, Thompson underlines the ambivalent power of religion. A significant portion of Bangladesh's education system is carried out by madrasas, religious schools that are either state-reformed (Aliya madrasas) or more traditional (Quomi madrasas). While in the past madrasas were mostly attended by boys only, recent years have seen the establishment of female madrasas as well. It is not always clear, however, whether these madrasas help to empower girls or actually serve to perpetuate traditional gender stereotypes. Recent studies found that compared to their counterparts at government schools, female students at madrasas have less positive views on increasing economic and educational opportunities for women, while also favouring larger families (Adams 2015; cf. Asadullah, Amin & Chaudhury 2019).

One of the key factors in faith engagement against child marriage is religious leaders. Again, religious leaders can use their moral authority in one way or the other. Since religious leaders not only interpret the Holy Scriptures and thereby help to shape social norms and values, they are also the ones performing the marriage rites, so gaining their support in combatting child marriage is crucial. "There is ample evidence that religious leaders can be critical allies in the fight to end early marriage, for example, by participating in campaigns aimed at ending the practice, collaborating with development actors, making public commitments, and refusing to perform or support the marriage" (Thompson 2020: n.p.).

While gender inequality plays out in all dimensions of religion, the following aspects are of particular importance.

Religion as Teachings: Cementing or Contesting Traditional Gender Roles

Religious teachings, in oral or written form, play a major role in defining social spaces and in cementing patriarchal settings. At the same time, however, religious teachings can also become the source for contesting traditional gender roles and for empowering women. This is clearly visible in the case of the SBC discussed above. Gender roles in SBC have long been defined by so called "complementarianism". "The ideology of complementarianism asserts that while women and men are equal in creation, they are distinct in function. Men are to serve as leaders of church and home; women are to support and submit to them" (Maxwell 2021: n.p.). This idea is based on the notion of "biblical womanhood" which in turn is rooted in a specific interpretation of certain passages in the Bible, prominent among them is 1 Corinthians 14:34: "Your women, let them be silent in the assemblies". Different hermeneutical approaches, however, that combine a historical-critical reading of the text with power sensitive perspectives allow for a different reading of such passages. Influential female leaders like Beth Moore challenge the practice of the so-called prooftexting, i.e. taking a passage out of context and applying a literal understanding to it. Instead, other readings emerge that emphasise justice and gender equality and invite us to revisit the Bible's view of women, for instance, through the lens of *Jesus Feminist* (this is the title of Bessey 2013).

Religion as Practice: Transforming Rituals and Traditions

Gender inequality is perhaps most easily visible in practices, rituals, and traditions. It is encountered in child marriages, in sending or not sending girls to school, in the way girls and women are able to publicly voice their opinions. Specific practices give concrete shape to the social, cultural, and religious spaces of the female half of humanity. Among the horrendous practices that illuminate gender inequality is FGM. As with many other harmful practices, FGM combines social, cultural, and religious aspects. It can be viewed as a purification ritual, as a kind of chastity belt, as preparation for marriage, as a time of celebration for the neighbourhood. Deeply rooted traditions cannot be changed overnight. Nor is simply adjusting legislation likely to be fruitful if it cannot be enforced. Sudan, for instance, outlawed FGM in 1947, yet continues to struggles with this practice. While this battle must be fought on many fronts, including legislation, education, and the willingness and patience to engage with women on the ground, religion is one of its key elements to either reinforce this practice or counter it. Edna Adan Ismail, one of the leading global advocates against FGM in Muslim countries worldwide, points to the importance of making clear that FGM is not a religious requirement in Islam. Talking about religious leaders in Somaliland, she recounts how she organised theological engagement with this topic. "They were able to talk to theologians, so they did not have to take my word for it. That's how I was able to convince them that indeed FGM was not in any way required by Islamic teachings". And she points to the productivity of her strategy: "It was very successful" (Adan Ismail, in Georgetown University Berkley Center for Religion, Peace & World Affairs 2013: n.p.).

Religion as Institutions: Engaging Faith Leaders for Gender Equality

As in many other development issues, religious leaders are key in addressing gender equality. Given the entanglement of the cultural, historical, and religious factors present here, religious leaders can provide a (re-)interpretation of specific scriptures in order to support the social and economic rights of girls and women. Islamic Relief (2019), for example, issued a guide entitled, "An Islamic human rights perspective on early and forced marriages" in order to demonstrate the consistency of Islamic core values with the importance of girl's health and education. A clear stance against child marriages is combined with an Islamic focus on "protecting the sanctity of marriage". On a local level, religious leaders have greater access on the ground and can personally communicate with families of at-risk girls. Especially in countries with religious education institutions, religious leaders can use their influence to call for a revision of textbooks to be more gender inclusive or to hire more female teachers. In Afghanistan, for example, World Vision has participated in training about 4,000 imams on gender equality, rights to education, and preventing violence against women and girls (VAWG). "As a result, Afghan faith leaders are reaching out to community groups, schools, military, and police to campaign against child marriage and for social justice" (World Vision 2022: n.p.).

Target 2 of SDG 5 aims at the elimination of all forms of violence against all women and girls in the public and private sphere. The following spotlight by Sandra Iman Pertek illustrates the role that Islam can play in both supporting and countering gender-based violence (GBV).

Spotlight: A Muslim Perspective on Gender Equality and Violence against Women and Girls (Sandra Iman Pertek)

In this reflection, I shed light on Islam, gender equality, and VAWG. I argue that there is a compelling Islamic case against gender injustice, but high illiteracy, conflict, and problematic exegesis compound gender inequality underpinning VAWG. General and religious illiteracy, entailing lack of awareness of women's rights, and gender inequalities go hand in hand. Varied religious interpretations can enable patriarchal cultural understandings of religious teachings. I first outline diverse Muslim gender perspectives, followed by exploring a Muslim case for gender equality and ending VAWG, and then discuss the status quo.

Diverse branches and schools of thought characterise Islam. Multiple individual, community, and structural factors shape Muslim approaches to women's issues, from what could be defined as "liberation" to what is often seen as "oppression", in other words from progressive to conservative views. Although some categories may appear binary, such as progressive and conservative perspectives, in reality, these are fluid and blurred as they mix and adapt to evolving conditions and social identities. For example, one may sustain progressive views on women's empowerment but remain conservative of their authority.

Diverse gender dynamics in faith communities originate from a context-specific understanding of the cosmological order, appearing to insiders as natural conditions of existence, which they reinforce as a product of these conditions in real life. Questioning gender inequalities from "within" communities is difficult as gender dynamics are normalised by communities socialised in such conditions. Despite Islam's strong anti-gender inequality and anti-VAWG message from the 7th century, as I outline below, ambiguous hermeneutics and socio-political conditions lead to diverse socially constructed religious manifestations which can reinforce gender inequality and VAWG.

A Muslim Case against Gender Inequality and VAWG

A Muslim case against gender inequality and VAWG is scriptural and relies on Islam's central text – the Qur'an – believed by Muslims to be a revealed word of God (in Arabic – *Allah*). Women and girls are addressed in the Islamic religious sources with numerous references made to their socio-economic rights, a dedicated Chapter 4 in the Qur'an (titled *al-nisa*, in English – women) and numerous *hadiths* (collections of the Prophet Muhammad's sayings/traditions).

For (non-exhaustive) scriptural illustration, social justice, human dignity and equality are commonly recognised as the key Qur'anic principles. Muslim activists and FBOs often use the scriptural equality of women and men in gender justice campaigns to challenge misconstrued gendered socio-religious interpretations. Examples include the Muslim adaptations of community-transformation methodologies – the Channels of Hope – by Islamic Relief Worldwide and World

Vision, and the transforming masculinities approach by Tearfund. Chapter 4, verse 135, for instance, is one of the most frequently cited Qur'anic verses calling Muslims against oppression. "O ye who believe! stand out firmly for justice, as witnesses to Allah, even as against yourselves, or your parents, or your kin, and whether it be (against) rich or poor" (Qur'an 4:135).

Similarly, Chapter 33, verse 35, challenges female exclusion from public life by addressing them on equal footing, as men, in compensating for their good deeds:

> For Muslim men and women, for believing men and women, for devout men and women, for true men and women, for men and women who are patient and constant, for men and women who humble themselves, for men and women who give in charity, for men and women who fast, for men and women who guard their chastity ... for them has Allah prepared forgiveness and great reward.
>
> *(Qur'an 33:35)*

Faith-inspired advocates often use the Qur'anic revelations, which outline women's rights to self-determination, to claim Islam theoretically emancipated women in revolutionary ways, centuries before feminist movements. Only in the last 30–40 years have Muslim scholars and Islamic feminists initiated an alternative narrative by reclaiming and reinterpreting religious texts (e.g. Mir-Hosseini et al. 2015; Ashrof 2005). On the premise that feminism and Islam are not mutually exclusive (Carland 2017), scholars challenge problematic hermeneutics, with the independent examination of religious sources (*ijtihad*) and reading of the Qur'an (*tafsir*). Since the original Qur'anic messaging was delivered and documented in Arabic, often offering pluralistic meanings, some exegeses have scope to distort the divine revelations. Some most problematic interpretations of hadiths relate to women's leadership, ability to file witness statements, and refuse intimate relations with a spouse. These and other narrations, to a contested degree of authenticity, contribute to discriminatory attitudes to women.

To counter patriarchal misbeliefs, campaigners utilise scriptural references to support women's rights to access work and education (Qur'an 96:1–5), own earnings and finance, manage inheritance (Qur'an 4:7), property and land rights (Qur'an 4:29), and preserve the family name. In addition, they promote female role models – Muslim women leaders – contributing to society from across Islamic civilisations. Paradoxically, although over half of religious sources were narrated by women, most by Ayesha (wife of Prophet Muhammad), women's authority remains undermined across patriarchal societies.

Moreover, Muslim educators often resort to the Prophet Muhammad (PBUH) as a central figure of Islam and the best example of a women's rights advocate, who demonstrated immense support and respect to women of Mecca and Medina. In his final sermon, he challenged patriarchy by reminding men that all humans are equal in the eyes of God and women have rights over men too. "O People, it is true that you have certain rights with regard to your women, but they also have rights over you ... Do treat your women well and be kind to them, for they are your partners and committed helpers" (narrated by Imam Ahmad, Hadith no. 19774, in ed. Al-Khattab 2012).

During the sermon, he also addressed the intersecting nature of gender discrimination and highlighted the racial equality between people, stating that people differentiate based on their virtues and not race. "All humans are descended from Adam and Eve, there is no superiority of an Arab over a non-Arab, or of a non-Arab over an Arab, and no superiority of a white person over a black person or of a black person over a white person, except on the basis of personal piety and righteousness" (narrated by Imam Ahmad, Hadith no. 19774, in Al-Khattab 2012).

It is also important to recognise that religious faith plays out in the lived experiences of VAWG survivors differently. Overall, religion operates as a source of resilience to abuse. For example, Syrian refugee women I met in Turkey prayed for protection from their oppressors. They drew upon their religious resources to cope with violence through cognitive, behavioural, and spiritual strategies (Pertek 2022). On the one hand, many found spiritual empowerment and relief in their prayers, on the other, endurance and trust in destiny perhaps deferred them from seeking help. I now discuss how religion can be instrumentalised locally to justify VAWG.

Instrumentalising Religion

The experiences of VAWG are shaped by internal and external intersecting religious influences (Pertek 2022). I highlight one of the most common internal drivers of VAWG across Muslim faith communities – the contentious interpretation of a Qur'anic verse, verse 34 of Chapter 4, which offers a pathway for family conflict resolution. The varying interpretations of this verse – particularly the word *"idrabihunna"*, commonly translated as 'hitting' – has not only generated much controversy, but also enabled abusers to justify their behaviours (Pertek 2022). However, the survivors (whom I met during my PhD data collection in Ankara) themselves point to references prohibiting domestic violence, recalling the prophetic message to treat women kindly with honour. For example, one woman in her interview mentioned, "The prophet said: 'Take my advice with regard to women: Act kindly' ... If the woman did something wrong, then religion says: '[A woman] must be retained in honour or released in kindness'" (Zainab, Syrian refugee, in Pertek 2022).

Nevertheless, the ambiguity of religious understandings continues to be misused to sanction women and enforce discriminatory family laws, particularly concerning inheritance, polygamy, and age of marriage. Certain methodologies of interpreting sacred texts, wider values, and contextual influences can enable women's subordination. Therefore, I consider such discriminatory processes a form of spiritual violence by violating one's relationship with the divine and infringing on one's belief system. Currently, following the trend of the #MeToo campaign and scandals of sexual violence in the Catholic Church, there is a similar growing movement manifesting in Muslim communities, where victims are disclosing incidents involving prominent religious figures. In response, new movements and projects against spiritual violence, such as the Hurma Project (2019) by Ingrid Mattson, encourage Muslims to tackle VAWG through Islamic ethics. Such movements often face backlash in faith communities, especially when associated with stigmatised notions of feminism. Public awareness-raising of the Islamic pro-women ethics is needed to ensure that women's rights, enshrined in the Islamic tradition, are better understood. I now consider further why the prevalence of VAWG prevails.

Religion vs Gender Inequality and VAWG

Translating Islam's gender ethics into real-life remains challenging in the Muslim world, as suggested by the sustained high gender inequality rates (cf. UNDP 2022). Lived religious experiences do not exist in a vacuum and are constantly renegotiated in the social world. Religious expressions intersect with (affecting and being affected by) multifarious factors, from geo-political, socio-economic conditions and patriarchal customs to evolving hermeneutics, which shape the conditions in which gender equality can be exercised contextually. Also, as religion relies on subjective experiences and feelings, certain ideas remain deeply entrenched. For example, some associate gender norms with divine orders, intertwining gender and religion daily. Thus, religious teachings may be misused based on the patriarchal cultural interpretations of texts taken out of context and personal interests.

In addition, widespread Islamophobia and presenting Muslim women as oppressed and Muslim men as oppressive misogynists complicate framing inequality and VAWG in Islam. Such binary perspectives put gender justice debates in the spotlight, compounding violence against Muslim women and discouraging victims from reporting abuse to protect their religion's image. In particular, debates on religious attire, especially Muslim women's head coverings, raise public controversies, depicting Muslim women as powerless and lacking agency. Their choices and expressions of religious identity are questioned, denying fundamental rights and clothing choices. Moreover, discriminatory laws deprive Muslim women of employment opportunities. Subsequently, Islamophobia reinforces VAWG based on the intersecting – religious, racial, and gender – discrimination.

Finally, I turn attention to how conflicts intensify patriarchal power imbalances, religious (mis)interpretations, and VAWG. We often hear about a backlash against women's rights, unsurprisingly in the conflict-torn Muslim world, where politicised, co-opted, and misogynist religious expressions grow as a weapon of war to gain control. In practice, integrating gender, conflict, and religious analysis is likely to produce more effective VAWG strategies. In addition, for lasting change, ending illiteracy is a crucial steppingstone to end VAWG through increasing faith awareness of women's rights, dismantling misconceptions, and transforming intergenerational gender norms. Finally, VAWG practitioners need to account for local Muslim women's voices on the roles of religion in their lives to contextualise and adapt their responses effectively.

9
"I HAVE A DREAM" – RELIGION MATTERS FOR THE REDUCTION OF INEQUALITY (SDG 10)

Introduction

The COVID-19 pandemic brought forth a number of negative records. Here is yet one more. The year 2020 marked the steepest increase in global billionaires' share of wealth on record, according to the World Inequality Report (WIR) (Chancel et al. 2022: 20). Since 1995, the share of global wealth owned by billionaires has increased from 1% to now over 3%. This means that the world's richest 1% own twice as much as the bottom 90%. And there is injustice even in injustice because it is far more men holding wealth than women. Globally, men possess 50% more in wealth than women, as a report by Oxfam finds (Oxfam International 2020).

Not only is global wealth unequally distributed, but income inequalities also abound. The poorest half of the global population earn 8.5% of the global income, while the richest 10% currently take 52%. And one more aspect sticks out: Inequality is also distributed unequally. The MENA (Middle East and North Africa) region is the most unequal region in the world, while Europe has the lowest inequality levels. In terms of personal discrimination, almost one in five people have personally experienced discrimination on at least one of the grounds prohibited under international human rights law (UNDESA n.d.; cf. SDG 10), according to data from 44 countries and territories for the period 2014–2020. This data also show that women were more likely to become victims of discrimination than men. Moreover, the number of refugees globally has reached its highest level on record, with the war in the Ukraine adding millions to the numbers of both internally displaced people and people forced to leave their home countries.

With inequalities that pronounced, we will not be able to address the challenges of the 21st century "without significant redistribution of wealth and income inequality" (Chancel et al., 2022: 20). SDG 10 therefore calls to "reduce inequality within and among countries". And some progress has indeed been made. Over the past decades, global inequalities between countries have declined. Before the pandemic, modest gains were made in "reducing income inequality in some countries and territories, continuing preferential trade status for lower-income countries and territories and decreasing transaction costs for remittances" (UNDESA n.d.; cf. SDG 10). Sending a $200 remittance cost 6.3% in 2021 as compared to 9.3% in 2011, bringing it closer to the international target of 5%. As we struggle for more equality on all levels, we also need to ask, what is the role of religion in all of this?

Religion and Human Rights: No Love at First Sight

All matters of inequality come together in the struggle for human rights. It therefore comes as no surprise that the foundational document of human rights, the Universal Declaration of Human Rights (UDHR), adopted in 1948, makes equality fundamental. Already the Preamble of the UDHR is a powerful witness to the equality of everyone, calling for the "recognition of the inherent dignity and of the equal and inalienable rights of all members of the human family" (UN 1948: para 1). This fundamental feature of the equality of all is then spelled out in different contexts, including equality in dignity and rights (Art. 1), equality before the law (Art. 7), equality of men and women, particularly regarding marriage (Art. 16), and equal pay for equal work (Art. 23).

When the UDHR was proclaimed by the United Nations General Assembly in Paris on December 10, 1948, it set out, for the first time, universal fundamental human rights. The UDHR then paved the way for the adoption of over 70 human rights treaties at a global and regional level. Drafted by representatives from different religious and cultural backgrounds, the UDHR was set against the experiences of the horrors of two world wars. There was acute awareness that national law by itself is insufficient for protecting the dignity of all. Rather, overarching standards are needed that every member of the human family can appeal to. In the struggle for human rights, religion has played a rather ambiguous role, however.

In the European context, the idea of human dignity at the root of human rights was influenced by the Greek-Roman tradition of Stoa, on the one hand, and the Christian tradition, on the other. While Cicero, for example, sees reason as foundational for human dignity, the Christian tradition points out that humans are created in the image of God (Gen 1:26) and that all humans are children of God (Gal 3:26–28). Despite these strong resources within the Christian tradition, Christian churches and theology for a long time had difficulties with the ideas of human dignity and human rights. These difficulties had partly theological reasons. The doctrine of original sin, for instance, was understood in a way as if sin had damaged human dignity. Other difficulties were based on political and social reasons such as the link between human rights and the French Revolution with its terror and its explicitly anti-church agenda. It was only the experiences of two world wars that would lead the churches and Christian theology to realise the necessity for universal human rights. Since then, especially the emerging global ecumenical movement and its conciliatory process for "Justice, Peace and Integrity of Creation" have become very fruitful for religious and interreligious human rights discourse and engagement.

Wanted: Religious Actors as "Immanent Critics" for Human Rights

The example of the historical development of the relationship between the Christian faith tradition and human rights yields two important lessons: First, human rights are *open to* different, particular foundations. From its inception, the UDHR included the insights and wisdom of different cultures and faith traditions. And second, human rights are *dependent on* different, particular foundations. Both lessons have far-reaching implications for human rights today. The idea of universal human rights needs to develop strong roots in each and every religious and non-religious tradition in order to avoid erosion. As a report by the Human Rights Watch puts it: "Human rights cannot truly go global unless it goes deeply local" (Marthoz & Saunders 2005: 2). We, as global citizens from vastly different religious and cultural backgrounds, therefore need to work out how our own specific tradition connects with human rights. This means, we need people who act as "immanent critics" (Michael Walzer) from within their own religious tradition, doing the theological and hermeneutical work necessary to show how human rights resonate with their own respective tradition. Granted, this might be a lot easier for some of the 30 rights encompassed by the UDHR than for others. Yet the fact that it might not be possible for all 30 rights for each and every particular tradition does not dispense from the struggle. There is a lot of common ground that has not yet been trodden. We all need to "own" human rights, yet without becoming exclusivist about it. Otherwise, human rights stand in danger of being perceived as something foreign, external, or "Western" (Schliesser 2021). In the following, we will see how the different dimensions of religion can be used – or misused – in the quest for equality and human rights.

Religion as Community: Exclusion and Embrace

Equality can also be framed in terms of participation and inclusion. And again, religion in terms of community can be used to exclude "the other", minorities, foreigners, etc. This happens oftentimes when religion is merged with the large community called the "nation state". In Pakistan, for example, "the creed of National Islamization has been used as a stick to beat all emancipatory and human rights movements", taking "a particularly heavy toll on the rights of women and religious minorities" (Jahangir 2000: 168f.). In a somewhat similar vein, the dramatic rise of Hindu nationalism in India resulted in a decline of minority rights as "the promotion and tolerance of attacks on women, Muslims, Christians, and Dalits has increased" (Chandra 2021: n.p.). At the same time, the community aspect of religion can serve to create relationships and support inclusion even across ethnic, religious, or national boundaries. One particular powerful example is the youth gathering at Rakvere's Karmeli Church in Estonia on April 16, 2022, in the middle of the ongoing war in Ukraine. This gathering, organised by the Baptist Church in Estonia, brought together young people from Estonia, Russia, and Ukraine in order to build community and relationships despite the divisions created by politics, culture, or language (Raihhelgauz 2022).

Religion as Practice: The Power of Non-violence and Love

Just as there are religiously inspired practices that support inequality, religious practices can also become potent sources in the struggle for equality and for human rights. One of these practices is non-violence. Mahatma Gandhi's struggle against the British Empire was famously characterised by a form of non-violence that Gandhi referred to as *satyagraha*, meaning "truth-force" or "love-force". Drawing on the Hindu cardinal virtue of *satya*, holding to truth and integrity, Gandhi connected *satya* with active and loving non-violence (Ardley 2003: 24f.). To practise satyagraha means seeking truth and love while refusing, through non-violent resistance, to take part in anything believed to be wrong. Gandhi connected the practice of satyagraha with other spiritual practices such as fasting as a way to purify oneself. Later, Gandhi's practice of non-violence inspired Martin Luther King Jr., whose "I have a dream"-speech of 1963 became a symbol for the struggle against racial inequality (Carson 2013). Martin Luther King Jr. connected Christianity to Gandhi's teachings. "I came to see for the first time that the Christian doctrine of love operating through the Gandhian method of non-violence was one of the most potent weapons available to oppressed people in their struggle for freedom" (King 1986: 38).

Religion as Institutions: Influential Allies for Human Rights

Religious institutions can be strongholds for harbouring and perpetuating inequality and gross human rights abuses. Prominent current examples include the discovery of abuse and deaths of hundreds of indigenous children by educational institutions operated by the Roman Catholic Church in Canada (Honderich 2021). At the same time, the institutional dimension of religion can become a powerful ally in the struggle for human rights. One example is the alliance of multiple religious organisations and institutions formed in the Jubilee 2000 campaign. Rooted in the Hebrew Bible's prescription (Lev 25) that at certain points in time economic relations should be reset, including the cancellation of debts and the returning of land and wealth, the Jubilee 2000 campaign advocated the cancellation of poor countries' debt. "The centrality of the religious frame drew faith-based organisations to the forefront of the campaign" (Freeman 2020: 66). Numerous religious institutions including the Vatican, different national councils of Catholic Bishops, the WCC, the Bishops of the Anglican Communion, and various FBOs and NGOs united in pushing for debt cancellation. And they did so with success. Eventually, in 1999 the G8 Cologne Summit adopted the HIPC-Initiative. Due to the HIPC-Initiative, about $70 billion of odious debts of 35 of the poorest countries were cancelled. This allowed these countries to focus their resources less on paying back debts to donor countries and more on sustainable developmental endeavours.

Religion as Framework: Transforming Mindsets

With its holistic perspective, encompassing the material and the spiritual, the cognitive and the emotional, religion is uniquely positioned to address issues that are deeply embedded in structures and cultures. This power can be wielded for good and for bad. The theological justification of the South African apartheid regime is one example of the perverted power of this *Weltanschauung* dimension of religion. At the same time, the very same Christian religion that was employed to justify structural human rights violations was turned to as a potent resource for critiquing the apartheid system. In 1982, The World Alliance of Reformed Churches under its South African leader Allan Boesak condemned the South African apartheid system as "sin". "We declare with black Reformed Christians of South Africa that apartheid ('separate development') is a sin, and that the moral and theological justification of it is a travesty of the Gospel" (quoted in de Gruchy & Villa-Vicencio 1983: 170). Human Rights Watch points to various civil rights movements that were powerfully inspired by religion. "The role U.S. and English Protestant churches in the anti-slavery campaigns, in the Congo reform movement, and in solidarity with Armenian victims in the late days of the Ottoman Empire belong to the best chapters of the history of the human rights movement" (Marthoz & Saunders 2005: 5). And even today, it is a religious figure – the Dalai Lama – who is prominently guiding the Tibetans' ongoing quest for freedom.

Pauline Kollontai's spotlight from a Jewish perspective will now serve to highlight the role of Judaism in the context of democracy and minority rights in Israel.

Spotlight: A Jewish Perspective on Democracy and Minority Rights in Israel (Pauline Kollontai)

Context

In 1948, the Founding Declaration of the Establishment of Israel stated that Israel is a sovereign Jewish and democratic state, and that its values are "based on freedom, justice and peace as envisaged by the Prophets of Israel", and will be implemented through "complete equality of social and political rights to all Israel's inhabitants irrespective of religion, race or sex" (Ben-Gurion 1948: 3). Statistics at the end of 2020 show that Israel has a Jewish majority population of 6.8 million, an Arab population of 1.95 million (Muslim Arabs are 1.88 million; Christian Arabs are 61,330), and a non-Arab population of 459,000 (Israel Central Bureau of Statistics [ICBS] 2020).

Israeli Arab Community

Both Muslim and Christian Arabs have their own autonomous education systems, and own and operate hospitals and nursing homes. Both have freedom to practise their religion in public. Arab local authorities manage Arab towns but their presence in Israeli state departments and ministerial offices remains extremely low. In comparison with the economic and educational situation of Jewish citizens there are significant inequalities for the Arab community; the gap between them and Jews has widened and the poverty rate amongst Israeli Arabs is four times higher than of Israeli Jews.

The Status of Human and Minority Rights

During the 1980s, work began on the development of two new Basic Laws that addressed human rights. In 1992, Knesset passed *The Basic Law on Human Dignity and Liberty (BLHDL)* and *The Basic Law on Freedom and Occupation*. The BLHDL was important as its central aim is "to protect human dignity and liberty of all Israel's citizens" (Knesset *BLHDL* 1992: Sec. 1). Minority rights received official attention during 2003–2004 as part of discussions headed up by the Constitution, Law and Justice Commission (CLJC) on the drafting of a written Constitution. Awareness of the vulnerability of Israel's minority groups was evident. However, there has been no further official consideration of this issue.

Focus: Religious Rights for Israel's Arab Minority

Freedom and protection for all Israeli citizens to practise their religion is recognised by the state and supported by criminal law. Despite these legal provisions, the number of religiously motivated attacks on Israel's non-Jewish communities has risen since 2006. Attacks are carried out mainly by Jewish religious youths connected to fundamentalist groups within the Orthodox and *Haredi* communities such as *Arvut Hadadit* (Mutual Responsibility). Other Jewish fundamentalist organisations such as *Gush Emunim* (Block of Faithfulness) propagate ideas and beliefs based on their "Greater Land of Israel" exclusionist ideology.

Attacks range from physical and verbal attacks on Muslim and Christian clerics and lay people, damage to their personal properties, damage to churches, mosques, cemeteries, and other holy sites. In more extreme attacks there has been loss of life. In January 2016, the complex of the Dormition Abbey of the Orthodox Church of Jerusalem was vandalised, and graffiti painted in red on walls saying, "Christians go to hell", and "Christians the enemies of Israel", which was accompanied by a Star of David. In 2018, Muslim women wearing hijab were verbally and physically abused in East Jerusalem. In January 2020, a mosque in the Sharafat area of East

Jerusalem was set on fire and anti-Muslim slogans painted on the walls. State-backed interference concerning ownership and use of Muslim and Christian holy places and non-religious property also occurs. In 2016, the "Nature and Parks Authority demolished 12 gravestones in the Muslim Bab al-Rahmeh cemetery because the gravestones lay in an expanded area of the cemetery that Israel considers a national park" (United States Office of International Religious Freedom [USOIRF] 2016: 44). In 2017, the Greek Orthodox Patriarchate (GOP) petitioned the Jerusalem District Court (JDC) contesting the forced transfer of church property rights of three of their buildings to a Jewish religious-Zionist organisation, Ateret Cohanim, populating East Jerusalem neighbourhoods with Jewish residents. The local court rejected the GOP petition, and it was subsequently rejected by Israel's Supreme Court (Surkes 2019: 1). The case was reopened in November 2019, but the Court again ruled in favour of Ateret Cohanim (Staff 2020).

Justification by Israeli Jewish fundamentalists for attacks are based on the biblical idea of the Promised Land given by God to the Israelites (Gen 15:15–2; Josh 1:4–7). They believe modern day Israel is the new manifestation of this Promised Land and that it is only for Jews. Their arguments for total rule of the land of Israel and the subjugation of Israel's non-Jews are further justified by appealing to texts from the Books of Deuteronomy and Numbers where the ancient Israelites are commanded to occupy all of Canaan and dispose of its existing inhabitants (Deut 20:12–18; Num 33:50–53). Some Jewish fundamentalists also use a basic tenant of *Kabbalah* (Jewish mysticism) that the Jewish soul and body are superior to the non-Jewish soul and body.

Challenging Jewish Fundamentalists

Jewish teachings of *Va'havtem et ha-Ger* (love of stranger) and *Ve'ahabhath le-re'akha* (love of neighbour) are central to challenging Jewish fundamentalists. The duty and responsibility to care for and love the stranger appear 36 times in the Hebrew Scriptures. Examples of these can be found in Leviticus 19:33–34, "When a stranger resides with you in your land, you shall not wrong him. The stranger who resides with you shall be to as one of your citizens; you shall love him as yourself". Further teachings on this issue are found in Leviticus 23:22, 24:22, and in Exodus 22:21. The importance of not oppressing the stranger appears in Exodus 23:9; practising justice towards the stranger is specified in Deuteronomy 24:18; and unjust treatment is identified as a serious violation of God's commands in Deuteronomy 27:19. Other teachings provide a code of behaviour between neighbours. Examples are found in the Ten Commandments (Exod 20:1–17). In Leviticus, the importance of treating a neighbour fairly and not perverting justice is stated (Lev 19:15). Treatment of stranger and neighbour are encapsulated in the command, "Thou shalt love thy neighbour as thyself" (Lev 19:18). Disregard for love of neighbour could have serious consequences and result in God's punishment according to 2nd century Rabbinic thought (ARNA. 16). Some Jewish scholars argue that the neighbour teachings apply only to Jews, but others, including Rabbi Ben Azzai (2 CE), Rabbi Hirschensohn, an Orthodox Zionist (1857–1935), and Rabbi Hammer (1933–2019), believe the concept of neighbour to be applicable to Jews and non-Jews.

Examples of how these teachings towards stranger/neighbour are being practised in Israel today are seen in the work of Rabbis for Human Rights (RHR) and *Tag-Meir* (Light Tag) (TM). RHR founded in the 1980s consists of Israeli rabbis and rabbinical students from different streams of Judaism. RHR's work focuses on Palestinian rights in the Occupied Territories and the rights of the Bedouin community located in the Negev. RHR do human rights work, legal advocacy/intervention, and engage in non-violent protests. In the run up to the 2015 Israeli election, RHR released several public statements identifying the teachings of love of stranger as Jewish responsibilities that they stated are an essential aspect to voting.

TM is an umbrella organisation founded in 2011 comprising of individuals and organisations across the religious and secular spectrums to advocate and implement the Jewish values of openness, tolerance, and respect for all Israelis as well as promote interreligious understanding. TM seeks to help victims of racism and violence amongst Israel's minorities through advocacy, legal help, material support, and holding vigils. Demonstrations, meetings, and other activities to raise public awareness are used to challenge the general public and government on rights violations. In reaction to the burning of the mosque in Sharafat in 2020, members of TM took a group of over 200 Jews to the burned-out mosque to meet the Imam and residents of the neighbourhood to express their condemnation of the attack, their feelings of shame, and to offer help with the clean-up and renovations.

Conclusion

The track record of the Israeli state shows that promotion and protection of the rights of its minority communities has been insufficient, and in recent years has significantly deteriorated. This is a product of a dominant Jewish Orthodox standpoint which disrespects Jewish teachings on care for stranger and neighbour, and exists alongside the fluctuating levels of Israel's liberal democracy, which has undergone a significant shift since 2006 to the political right. However, examples such as RHR and TM show not only how the constructive resources of religion become visible, but they also demonstrate that significant parts of civil society are not willing to succumb to sacralised right wing ideology.

10
"GREEN RELIGION" – RELIGION MATTERS FOR CLIMATE ACTION (SDG 13)

"Woefully Off Track"

"Woefully off track to stay at or below 1.5°C as called for in the Paris Agreement" (UNDESA 2022: n.p.). This is the sober reality described by the SDG Report 2021. In 2020, the global average temperature was 1.2°C above the pre-industrial baseline. The years 2015 to 2020 are likely to be the warmest years on record. After a temporary reduction in emissions of major greenhouse gases in reaction to the COVID-19 pandemic, the atmospheric concentration of these gases continues to increase. Climate change not only affects our planet's climate, its temperature, water and air, but also has sweeping consequences. Climate change makes the achievement of many other SDGs less likely. At the same time, nations around the world seem to become aware of the urgency of these issues as they also feel the push of voters and youth movements such as "Fridays for Future". The national election in Germany in 2021, for example, was dominated by issues around climate change, with Germany's Green Party emerging significantly strengthened.

Additionally, some progress has been made in taking "urgent action to combat climate change and its impacts", as SDG 13 calls for. By the end of 2020, 189 countries and territories plus the EU had issued a nationally determined contribution to the United Nations Framework Convention on Climate Change (UNFCCC). The UNFCCC secretariat was established in 1992 and supports the global response to climate change. The Convention is the parent treaty of both the Paris Agreement of 2015 and the Kyoto Protocol of 1997, and with 197 participating parties, it has near universal membership. Further progress is being made in climate financing. Compared to 2015–2016, climate finance increased by 10% to $48.7 billion in the period 2017–2018. Yet "to limit global warming to 1.5°C above pre-industrial levels in accordance with the Paris Agreement, the world would need to achieve net zero carbon dioxide emissions by around 2050"

DOI: 10.4324/9781003332275-13

(UNDESA 2022: n.p.). This, in turn, requires not only cosmetic adjustments, but a radical re-thinking of economies, industry, consumption, and individual lifestyles. Nothing less than a new vision of the common good and of the world we want is required, and this is the cue for religion.

Green for God? A Brief History of Religion and the Environment

On September 8, 2021, for the first time, the leaders of three major Christian churches – the Roman Catholic Church, the Eastern Orthodox Church, and the Anglican Communion – issued a joint appeal ahead of the UN Climate Change Conference COP26 in Glasgow, UK. In their statement, the Christian leaders warned of the urgency of climate change and its consequences on poverty. They called for global cooperation and promoted the concept of stewardship as an individual and collective responsibility for our planet and for social, economic, and environmental sustainability. Calling for a different lifestyle, the religious leaders proclaim: "We have maximized our own interest at the expense of future generations. By concentrating on our wealth, we find that long-term assets, including the bounty of nature, are depleted for short-term advantage" (UN Climate Change 2021: n.p.).

Does this sentiment reflect a newly found enthusiasm for environmental concerns? Or has religion always been "green for God" (cf. Carlisle & Clark 2018)? Quite on the contrary, says historian Lynn White Jr. According to White, Western Christianity in particular carries a "burden of guilt" for the environmental crisis we are facing today. For Western, Christianity has been instrumental in desacralising and instrumentalising nature to human ends (White 1967). White further criticises that the command in the Book of Genesis to "subdue the earth" (Gen 1:25) has been used to justify unrestrained environmental exploitation and destruction. It seems that White is onto something here, even though the subject matter might be a bit more complex than how White presents it. While the demystification and desacralisation of our modern life-world certainly has several roots – not least the Enlightenment and Kant's well-known admonition *sapere aude* ("dare to know") – White rightly points to a problematic hermeneutics long prevalent in Christian interpretation of the Book of Genesis. Only gradually has God's command to "subdue the earth" been understood less in terms of exploitation but rather as responsible stewardship. And only slowly is an individualistic, anthropocentric perspective being replaced by a concern for God's entire creation. Yet the theological perspectives on the environment were never unified, as alternative voices such as St. Francis of Assisi (1181 or 1182–1226) show. His "Canticle of the Sun" inspired Pope Francis and his influential encyclical *Laudato si'* in 2015, the first-ever papal encyclical devoted to the environmental crisis. It thus took centuries for insights such as the ones put forth by St. Francis to gain a stronger foothold. Here, the worldwide ecumenical movement has played a decisive role in putting the environment on the theological agenda. In 1986, the

6th Assembly of the WCC in Vancouver agreed to engage in a conciliar process of mutual commitment for "Justice, Peace and the Integrity of Creation", a process that is still ongoing today.

Just as Christianity, other religions also incorporate a wide array of perspectives on environment issues and climate change. Within Islam, for example, rather different interpretations of climate change are being offered (Koehrsen 2021: 5). They range from understanding climate change as caused by humans and as the consequence of the current economic system and lifestyles, to assigning spiritual causes that see climate change as part of God's punishment for sinful behaviour, or as a sign of the approaching end-of-times. Still other Muslim perspectives reject climate change altogether as a Western product of imagination designed to weaken the Muslim world. While climate change sceptics are at home in many different religions, most faith traditions seem to have accepted climate change as human-made. Many have thus formed intra- and inter-faith coalitions and have issued statements for the protection of the environment (cf. the Buddhist Declaration on Climate Change, A Rabbinic Letter on the Climate Crisis, Islamic Declaration on Global Climate Change, the encyclical *Laudato si'*, all released in 2015).

To sum up, for centuries, the religious resources for environmental care remained mostly hidden in different religious traditions. Their systematic recovery has significantly increased only in the 1980s/1990s and continues to gain traction. So is religion in general becoming greener? Yes and no. Yes, because – with environmental problems becoming ever more pressing – many religions step up their theological reflection and practical engagement with environmental issues. And no, because on the one hand, many theological resources for environmental care have always been there, yet need to be rediscovered and made fruitful. And no, because on the other hand, religion does not exist in a vacuum, but religious actors always interact with their concrete setting. In this way, their environmental concern is also "a reflection of the sociocultural context in which these individuals are situated" (Carlisle & Clark 2018: 235).

"Together United" – Inter-faith Engagement for the Environment

Before the UN Climate Change Conference COP26 in Glasgow in 2021, about 40 religious leaders from different faith traditions issued a joint appeal – following the similar statement by the leaders of the three Christian churches mentioned above. In their pre-COP26 appeal, the religious leaders stress the commonalities between their faith traditions with regards to environmental concerns. "We come together united to raise awareness of the unprecedented challenges that threaten our beautiful common home. Our faiths and our spiritualities teach a duty to care for the human family and for the environment in which it lives" (UNFCCC 2021: n.p.). While this appeal focuses on the commonalities across different faith traditions, it draws on the theological work done within each individual religion. This hermeneutical work examines critically and self-critically axioms on humans' relationship with creation and humans' position within creation. With religion being ever ambivalent, its potent resources for countering a destructive mindset and exploitative action wait to be put to use.

The following overview gives a very brief glimpse of selected eco-theological resources in different faith traditions. In Islam, for instance, the concepts of "oneness of God" (*tawhid*), pointing to the unity of humans and nature in creation, and "inviolate zone" (*hima*), a piece of land set aside for spiritual purposes as well as the admonition to avoid waste (Sura 7:31), are found to be helpful in developing an Islamic pro-environmental ethics. According to Bagir and Martiam (2016), however, it is the idea of stewardship (*khalifa*) that is most productive for Islamic environmentalism. The idea embedded in the term *khalifa* conveys that God entrusts humans with the responsibility of caring for his creation (Bagir & Martiam 2016: 81; Koehrsen 2021: 3). Buddhism, on the other hand, teaches the interconnectedness of all things great and small. If earth is harmed, humans are harmed as well. Buddhism therefore encourages balance in all respects of life in order to repair the broken relationship between humanity and nature (Dalai Lama 1992). Echoing sentiments in other faith traditions, Yudhistir Govinda Das of the International Society for Krishna Consciousness (Iskcon) points to the root problem of climate change: "Our greed and propensity to exploit others (including nature). This is the root cause of the issue" (Govinda Das, cited in Chanda-Vaz 2020: n.p.). Besides norms and concepts, stories are also powerful resources for eco-spirituality. Representatives of the Pacific Islands, for example, present a particularly strong narrative when speaking about the environmental fate their islands are facing. "It is more than entire households and livelihoods and cultures being submerged in a few years' time. … It is about our ancestors' bones being washed away" (UNFPA 2014: 37). Spiritual narratives like this one can be very inspirational for encouraging the paradigm shifts necessary on all levels.

Based on their own respective potent resources for countering climate change (for a helpful overview on different religions' perspectives on ecological issues, cf. PaRD 2016), many religions engage not only in intrareligious, but also in interreligious dialogue and diapraxis for the environment. Yet with many faith traditions contributing individually and jointly to countering climate change, the question inevitably rises how exactly religions go about it. The following dimensions of religion can be helpful in better understanding the nature of these contributions.

Religion as Teachings: Integral Ecological Education

The role of integral ecological education in religious educational and cultural institutions around the world can hardly be overestimated. Again, the effects of religious teachings on environmental issues can be for good or bad. While the Christian misinterpretation of Genesis 1:25 ("subdue the earth") is an example of the latter, Pope Francis' encyclical *Laudato si'* or the Islamic Declaration on Global Climate Change (IFEES 2015), both released in 2015 along with statements of other religious traditions, provide constructive teachings on eco-theology. Yet education imparts not only important cognitive knowledge and concepts, but also works on a deeper level through the formation of norms and values. This is particularly important in this context, for as Iranian-American philosopher Seyyed Hossein Nasr (1997: 12) observes, "the environmental crisis is fundamentally a crisis of values". And since religions are a significant source of values in many cultures, they play a major role in influencing people's attitudes and actions towards the environment. Religious values, for instance, can be potent enough to override differences in other areas. As one recent study shows, religion can help to bring people together for the purpose of environmental protection, even across vast political divides. "Highly religious conservatives tend less to make liberals 'the other,' or at least religious liberals with whom they share a number of values, and thus are more open to embracing pro-environmental attitudes. Therefore, contradictions and antagonisms, such as the liberal versus conservative debate on anthropogenic environmental problems, can be resolved by increased religiosity" (Hekmatpour 2020: 17).

Religion as Spirituality: Eco-Spirituality as a Way of Life

#LaudatoSiLent. Initiated by the Laudato Si' Movement, this hashtag signalled a period of fasting related to climate change in 2021. Like many other religious climate movements, this movement (formerly known as Global Catholic Climate Movement) was born in 2015, in the wake of the Paris Climate Agreement. Believers and non-believers alike were challenged to fast during Lent, the liturgical season of 40 days preceding Easter. However, rather than rejecting the intake of food and drink, #LaudatoSiLent proposed for each week of Lent a different area of our Western lifestyles for fasting such as buying, eating meat, or being silent on environmental matters. Fasting, as a form of spiritual self-denial, is meant to support a change of heart and mind and to reassess one's priorities. "Christian spirituality proposes ... the capacity to be happy with little" (Pope Francis 2015: §222).

In a similar vein, religious actors from other traditions creatively draw on the spiritual resources of their faiths in addressing climate change. Muslim climate activists in the UK, for instance, create "Green Prayers" (Nita 2014) by combining traditional Muslim structure and form of prayer with pro-environmental content. The Buddhist Centre in Oslo initiated an interreligious climate pilgrim from Oslo (cf. All Triratna n.d.). And artists like Susan Seddon Boulet express their eco-spirituality in shamanic paintings featuring the interconnectedness of all species (Babcock 2016). All initiatives and actors are joined by the conviction that human flourishing encompasses both material and spiritual dimensions. This holistic understanding of human nature in turn impacts our way of life and our everyday choices.

Religion as Practice: Sustainable Lifestyles

"Practice what you preach". This basic admonition holds true in all contexts, yet the effects are especially visible regarding the environment and climate change.

Areas of practice and action are manifold and include, as the Joint Appeal (UN Climate Change 2021: n.p.) points out, cooperation to "favour a transition to clean energy; adopt sustainable land use practices; transform food systems to become environmentally-friendly and respectful of local cultures; end hunger; and to promote sustainable lifestyles and patterns of consumption and production ... and to adopt responsible financing". Action on all levels is required, i.e. from the individual level to the level of local religious communities to regional, national, and international networks. And it does make a difference how religious players themselves act. The Vatican's total net assets in 2019 were about USD 4.65 billion (Pullella 2020). Other religious institutions such as the Church of Jesus Christ of Latter-day Saints (Mormon church) and the Church of England also reach a multi-billion-dollar net worth. So it does matter whether the goods purchased, the services hired, and the financial investments undertaken are in line with environmentally and socially responsible standards.

And numerous religious actors – individual and institutional – have already engaged in practices countering climate change, thereby leading by example and inspiring others to follow. Sikh leader Balbir Singh Seechewal, for example, also known as Eco Baba, is spearheading a campaign to save the Kali Bein river in Punjab from pollution. The Swiss initiative "10forFuture" connects individuals and church communities who want to reduce their carbon footprint and become climate neutral. Cambridge Central Mosque has already achieved a near-zero carbon footprint and is Europe's first eco-friendly mosque (cf. The Cambridge Mosque Trust n.d.). On the international level, inter-faith coalitions like GreenFaith address environmental issues holistically (cf. GreenFaith n.d.). And countless more initiatives worldwide give testimony to the growing numbers of religious actors engaged in practices countering climate change.

Religion as Framework: Climate Justice

Though less visible than religious practice or teachings, religion as framework is the underlying foundation from which everything else emanates. It is the blueprint for body, mind and soul, thought, and action. And countering climate change requires nothing less than a new blueprint for humanity, a radical transformation of the way we think, act and live. Thinkers from different faith traditions have identified human "greed and propensity to exploit others" (Govinda Das, cited in Chanda-Vaz 2020: n.p.) as the underlying cause for the climate crisis. Pope Francis (2015: §109) comes to a similar conclusion when he criticises the "technocratic paradigm [which] accepts every advance in technology with a view to profit, without concern for its potentially negative impact on human beings" and wherein "finance overwhelm[s] the real economy" of human flourishing. The term "climate justice" used by many religious actors makes the link between climate change and economic exploitation visible.

What is needed is a new framework, a new imaginary, a change of heart and mind. The morals of the more the better needs to be replaced by an ethics of enough is enough. In his interpretation of the first of the Ten Commandments, German reformer Martin Luther (1483–1546) explains: "Whatever your heart clings to is really your god" (Luther 1959: 367). And religions are very good at replacing "old gods" with a new god, and old perspectives with new visions, thereby changing perceptions which in turn can generate entire new lifestyles. Referring to the example of various pro-environment initiatives by Muslims in the UK that range from education to campaigning and activism, Gilliat-Ray and Bryant (2011: 303) conclude, "These projects signal the potential for faith-based initiatives that go beyond merely informing or educating, and might lead to the possibility of real changes in behaviour".

What a sustainable lifestyle can look like has been demonstrated for centuries by the indigenous people in the Great Lakes region of the United States of America. Traditional ecological knowledge and teachings combine to form sustainable ways of life in tune with the natural seasonal rhythms and tribal spirituality as the spotlight by John C. Rodwan illustrates.

Spotlight: An Indigenous Perspective on Traditional Ecological Knowledge and Climate Change (John C. Rodwan)

Seen through the lens of a traditional indigenous person residing in the Southern Great Lakes region (USA), environment and spirituality are indivisible and are typically not thought of as independent concepts. Traditional ecological knowledge was *earned* within indigenous communities through untold generations of observation, trial and error, and a sheer will to persist, all of which are underscored through the belief of a higher power. Natural resources are considered to be animate and subject to ceremony upon their use. Upon harvesting a fish or medicinal plant, for example, an offering and recognition to Gitchee Manitou, The Creator, is essential. A physical offering may be in the form of a pinch of tobacco (sema) when available, but always a brief thought or prayer of thanks is given.

Although words such as "environment" and "ecology" were not a part of the indigenous language, as they are constructs of conventional Western science, traditional ecological knowledge is rich in the understanding of the interconnectedness of nature. An extraordinary sense of the balance of natural resources within an indigenous community is a life-sustaining force. To unbalance natural resources would potentially pose a threat to the health and well-being of a community. Over-extraction or waste of natural resources would be offensive to The Creator and result in a sequence of negative consequences.

The primary elements of nature are considered to be Wind, Water, Earth, and Fire, all balanced and interrelated within a "Medicine Wheel". Within the primary elements, we find the four directions, the totem animals, and even the races of humanity, each represented by the colours white, black, yellow, and red. A complete understanding of the medicine wheel is not possible since it is based upon the infinitely complex fixed will of The Creator, but intergenerational oral teachings are provided throughout life from entry into the world in the east direction to leaving this world in the western direction. Elders, of course, hold the most knowledge. Elders within spiritual lodges or medicine societies can be the purveyors of advanced knowledge.

Elemental fire is a great importance since it provides the mechanism to more fully interrelate or speak-with The Creator. The smoke resulting from and being a part of fire carries messages upwards to be heard, understood, and acted upon by The Creator. While all fire is esteemed and understood as a base element, ceremonial fire is considered sacred and is started in a very specific manner by a firekeeper. Firekeepers are esteemed members of the community and are called upon for all manner of ceremony, including the passing of a member of the community (known as "walking on"). Ecologic fire may or may not be considered ceremonial since it is sometimes created through natural forces such as lightning. Ecologic fire can also be started by a firekeeper and used as a tool to manage the environment. Since much of the southern Great Lakes region was occupied by grasslands, oak savanna and prairies, the fire was programmed into its ecology. Grasslands themselves persisted due to their deep roots and tolerance of fire at regular intervals. Conversely, trees were generally intolerant of fire, therefore forests were less common in the region. In the grasslands, there was wildlife within the intricate web of life that was dependent upon the tender flora that grew from the burnt-over lands. Many of these creatures were important components of the indigenous lifeway, of which bison, deer, and small game were included and sustainably harvested.

Considering other observations of spirituality in the indigenous communities, I once asked an elder dressed in regalia preparing for a dance at a Traditional Pow Wow if he "made his staff". The staff was beautifully ornamented with coloured sinew, eagle feathers, rabbit fluff and pony beads all affixed to an extraordinary stick. Perhaps the question was rhetorical, meaning to extract the history of the staff which the bearer most certainly made or was given through kinship or gift. To my surprise, the elder simply replied with "no" and did not immediately expand upon this comment. Instead, the elder paused, then said, "The Creator made it and he had simply assembled it". This provided significant insight into the humility and spiritually of the indigenous lifeway.

Ceremony and prayer are an important component of food for the indigenous peoples of the region, as well as all areas populated by Anishinabek (a common reference for indigenous people when speaking of themselves or community members). As is common in many practices observed in Christian meals, the Anishinabek frequently "bless" or give thanks to seeds being planted, and plants and animals being harvested from the environment. As a preface to the serving of community meals, an elder is generally called upon to provide a blessing. An offering of sema is a typical practice upon making the request, as well as many other requests of elders. The spoken blessing nearly always refers to being thankful to The Creator for providing nourishment for their bodies and gathering of the community in a "good way".

Water holds a particularly prominent place in the Anishinabek lifeway. During pre-Euromerican contact, water served as the universal constant, providing the foundation of ecology as well as transportation, economy, fishing, and foraging, among others. Also, placing a pinch of sema into a flowing waterway is common following a community member passing on. The sema within the water is intended to request The Creator to provide a safe passage for the spirit into the afterlife. Regarding their own humanity, a woman's body holds special spiritual reverence due to foetus' being born from a woman's own water. Women are frequently provided a higher level of communal protection in order that their water is a safe haven for the growing of a foetus, therefore the continuation of the community. "Water ceremonies" are gender specific to women and are practiced when protection is a concern or the bonding of a community activity such as blessings conducted after the Winter Moons give way to the Spring Moons.

The concept of climate change is largely a Western tenet, with the Anishinabek tending to have the notion "when hasn't the climate been changing". This is not to say that climate change is not recognised, but rather, it is viewed more as a matter of a continuum of adaptation. As part of the Anishinabek creation story, there exists a constant series of adaptations throughout the span of time. The climate has had a general trend of warming and is now accelerated. The indigenous view of time tends not to be in years, but rather in generations.

Traditional ecological knowledge accounts for climate change, although it is not specifically referenced. It is understood by the community that certain natural resources have migrated to the southern Great Lakes. Wild rice is perhaps the most prominent example of sustenance adapting to a changing landscape. Teachings rightly indicate that wild rice originates at the eastern seaboard of North America, with it being known as Manoomin, translating directly to "the good berry". The good berry was placed on the water as an important feature of the region's habitat. The Bodewadmi ("the people") migrated in search of wild rice in response to messages from The Creator. Not only do the Anishinabek recognise wild rice as a central foodstuff, but also an essential component of food for the web of wildlife, particularly for waterfowl, since their southern migrations are during the time the wild rice ripens. It has been told that the bellies of migrating ducks were filled with wild rice, serving as a bonus for meals during the fall, which is a critical time for winter preparations. The Anishinabek are well aware of their origins and that they descended from a hunter and gatherer lifeway to an agro-nomadic lifeway, both with a degree of mobility. Even in the teachings of contemporary elders, references to seasonal food gathering encampments are well known. Berries and the gathering of maple sap from sugar-bush are important examples of seasonal mobility. Mobility is a primary tenet of humanity and of adapting to environmental change.

From the Anishinabek perspective, to abuse the land, the water, the air and the environment, is to abuse one's self. The Western model of environmental "management" is generally linear in practice. For example, land is acquired, its resources are harvested, its resources are depleted, then the ecosystem fails, and the land becomes devalued and unable to sustain a healthy lifeway. Linear thinking generally has negative consequences upon the environment. Through a compilation of linear approaches on a global scale, we witness human-caused and accelerated climate change. A holistic approach to environmental management is more likely to sustain both wildlife and humans; therefore adopting a circular, rhythmic approach to environmental management can only serve to slow climate change. When considering our lands, we would benefit from an Anishinabek approach that recognises the indivisible relationship with The Creator and the fully interconnected web of life that has been created.

11
"BROKERS OF PEACE" – RELIGION MATTERS FOR PEACE AND JUSTICE (SDG 16)

Peace and Justice as the Foundations of Development

While all of the SDGs are both vital and interconnected, it is SDG 16 that should actually stand at the beginning. For peace and justice are the foundations for everything else. If we don't have peace, our efforts for poverty alleviation, or quality education, or gender equality will remain severely limited. The Global Hunger Index points to this relationship by reporting that violent conflicts have become the biggest driving forces of hunger. "War and famine, two fearsome horsemen, have long ridden side by side ... The impact of all ... forms of violence on development is major and severe; the victims are poorer, more vulnerable and hungrier than others" (de Waal 2015: 23).

Currently, the vision promoted by SDG 16 of peaceful, just, and inclusive societies seems to come from a different universe. Millions of people have to live in fragile and conflict-affected contexts. The war in Ukraine has been interpreted as a change of times in many respects, including questions of defence and security, energy and economics both within Europe and beyond. Worldwide, state-based conflicts are at a historical high, as a 2022 Peace Research Institute Oslo (PRIO) report states. "In 2021, 54 state-based conflicts were recorded in 35 countries, resulting in nearly 85.000 battle-related deaths" (Palik et al. 2022: 9). At the same time, non-state conflicts stabilise at higher levels than previously recorded, while one-sided violence increases as well. With much of the world's attention being currently directed to the war in Ukraine, two worrisome trends must not be ignored. First, eight of the ten new conflicts are in Africa. Second, ISIS is involved in five of these new conflicts (Strand et al. 2020: 3). Given these trends and figures, it comes as no surprise that over the past few years, the number of people worldwide fleeing war, persecution, and conflict has been continuously rising. In this regard, the end of 2021 marked a new all-time high with 89.3 million people

(UN Progress and Info 2022), with the war in Ukraine leading to millions more. At the same time, for the past 20 years, the amount used for military expenditure has increased almost constantly, from USD 1.139 billion in 2001 to USD 2.023 billion in 2022 (Statista 2022).

There are some bright spots, however, as the global homicide rate has declined slowly from 6.3 per 100,000 people in 2015 to 5.9 per 100,000 in 2020. By 2021, access to information laws had been adopted by 127 countries, compared with 95 countries in 2013, thereby establishing the right of and procedures for the public to request and receive government-held information. In 2020, three more independently functioning national human rights institutions (NHRIs) were founded in sub-Saharan Africa and Europe, increasing the proportion of countries in compliance with the Paris Principles to 42%. While even small steps in the right direction are much appreciated, they illustrate at the same time the long road that is still ahead. Yet what has religion got to do with this?

Religion and Violent Conflict: Best Friends Forever?

The conflictive sides of religion are well known and religion's potential for inciting hatred and violence is easily visible in both past and present conflicts ranging from the Crusades to the 30-Years' War, the Northern Ireland Conflict, ISIS, and Northern Nigeria. As Charles Kimball (2002: 1) puts it, "It is somewhat trite, but nevertheless sadly true, to say that more wars have been waged, more people killed, and these days more evil perpetrated in the name of religion than by any other institutional force in human history". In order to gain a better understanding of violence, however, we need to take a brief look at its different dimensions. Here, the work of Norwegian peace researcher Johan Galtung is especially helpful. Galtung (1990) differentiates between three dimensions of violence, namely direct, structural, and cultural violence. In cases of direct violence, the perpetrator and victim can usually be clearly identified. Structural violence refers to violence ingrained in institutions, structures, or organisations. Examples of structural violence are discrimination or the unjust distribution of resources and opportunities. Both structural and direct violence is fed by cultural violence. This kind of violence is part of a community's "deep culture" (Galtung) nourished by foundational narratives, systems of values, and cultural memories. All three dimensions of violence are interrelated. And just as religion can serve to exacerbate violent conflict on all three levels, it can equally serve to transform violence in all its dimensions.

Some Terms: Conflict Resolution, Conflict Transformation, Peacebuilding, and Reconciliation

At this point, we need to very briefly look at the different vocabularies used in this field (cf. Schliesser 2020: 127–129). What is conflict resolution and how is it different from conflict transformation, peacebuilding, and reconciliation? Conflict resolution is the term most often encountered to describe discourses and activities aimed at ending (violent) conflict in a constructive manner. The concept of conflict transformation is connected with US peace scholar John Paul Lederach who relates peace to justice and brings in a focus on relationships next to content, and long-term transformations next to quick-fix solutions. Seeking to integrate peacekeeping, peacemaking, and peacebuilding, Johan Galtung, on the other hand, puts forward a comprehensive perspective on sustainable peace in his concept of peacebuilding that includes relationship and capacity building as well as bottom-up initiatives. Reconciliation then focuses on the healing of relationships and the (re-)establishment of trust after historical trauma by incorporating different elements such as the confession of guilt, remorse, asking and granting of forgiveness, truth finding and reparations (Schliesser 2018: 137–146).

Religion, as it turns out, can be a constructive, yet often neglected resource for all these endeavours. Furthermore, recent studies point in particular to the positive impact of religion in conflict prevention. "Faith-based approaches offer insights valuable to the wider conflict prevention field, which is increasingly critiqued for its liberal underpinnings and emphasis on technical and technological solutions" (Payne 2020: 1).

Religious Peacebuilding on the Rise

"[R]eligious groups ... have recently and collectively increased their peacemaking efforts" (Haynes 2007:69). Nevertheless, public perception and media portrayal of conflicts with a religious dimension usually focus on religion's destructive power. This is only one side of the story, however. "Religion is a source not only of intolerance, human rights violations, and extremist violence, but also of non-violent conflict transformation, the defence of human rights, integrity in government, and reconciliation and stability in divided societies" (Appleby 1996: 821). Recent years have seen growing interest on the side of academics, policymakers, and practitioners in the role of religion in conflict transformation and peacebuilding, and increasing efforts are invested in exploring the potent resources of religion for sustainable peace and reconciliation. As policy analyst Philippe Perchoc (2016: 1) points out in a briefing to the European Parliament, "International organisations, states and think-tanks are giving increasing consideration to the religious dimensions of conflict resolution". One indication of this rather recent attentiveness is the EU's first-ever appointment of a Special Envoy for the promotion of freedom of religion or belief outside the EU in 2016. This appointment testifies to the recognition of the link between freedom of religion, conscience, and thought on the one hand, and peace and stability on the other. "Violations of freedom of religion or belief may exacerbate intolerance and often constitute early indicators of potential violence and conflicts" (Council of the European Union 2013: 1).

While the role of religion in helping to transform conflicts must not be ignored, it should not be overestimated either. Just as religion is rarely the sole driving force behind violent conflict, but part of an intricate web that includes social, political, economic, and cultural factors, religion is rarely the one and only solution for creating peace. "Whether it is a direct or indirect dimension of the conflict, religion is part of the cultural matrix, and must be taken into consideration by brokers of peace. Bringing in religious actors or addressing religious questions is rarely sufficient for addressing the entire picture. Yet, engaging religion may have considerable potential when it opens up a new path to discuss fundamental assumptions held by conflicting groups, and as one out of several components in a peace process" (Harpviken & Røislien 2005: 17). The "considerable potential" of religion is sketched out in the following in terms of religion's different dimensions as they become relevant in this context.

Religion as Community: Building Constructive Relationships Across Boundaries

Faith actors engaged in peacebuilding oftentimes display a remarkable ability in terms of building relationships within and even across communities. "Religious leaders are uniquely positioned to foster non-violent conflict transformation through the building of constructive, collaborative relationships within and across ethnic and religious groups for the common good of the entire population of a region" (Appleby 2008: 127). The relationship-building talent of many religious peacebuilders is supported by the trust they enjoy in various contexts. This trust stems not least from the perception of religious actors as neutral and committed to the cause of peace only rather than seeking personal advantage (Bouta et al. 2005). Being trusted, respected, and well-networked puts religious peacebuilders in the position to function as "connectors" between different groups and communities. This is a vital competence in processes of conflict transformation where the dissemination and acceptance of new ways of thinking and behaving – for example, thinking in terms of a "new" framework of reconciliation instead of the "old" framework of revenge – is a crucial component for success.

Religion as Teachings: Love and Forgiveness vs. Hatred and Revenge

In volatile situations, this dimension of religion becomes all the more important. Religiously grounded normative concepts and values shape the way people think and act. Just as these teachings can unleash destructive forces, they can also be enormously productive for countering violence. It does make a difference whether love and forgiveness are being propagated or hatred and revenge. Living at the time of unabated Nazi terror, German pastor and Nazi resistance fighter Dietrich Bonhoeffer (2010: 49) draws on his Christian ethical convictions for his own engagement for the Jews and other minorities by arguing, "Inactive waiting and dully looking on are not Christian response. Christians are called to action and sympathy not through their own firsthand experiences but by the immediate experience of their brothers, for whose sake Christ suffered". Responsible action for peace and justice on behalf of the oppressed is understood here as mirroring the will of God. From this perspective, understanding one's own action in accordance with divine will can serve as a great force of motivation and orientation for peacebuilding.

Religion as Spirituality: Spiritual Care for the Wounded

Violent conflict leaves people wounded in body and soul. While physical scars fade over time, emotional wounds are invisible, yet can fester if left unattended. Feelings of powerlessness, bitterness, and hatred grow and feed into the spiral of violence, turning victims into perpetrators. Survivors of traumatic violence oftentimes struggle with integrating their experience into their own personal life narrative. Here, religious frameworks can help in providing meaning, such as offering an eschatological perspective of hope that transcends the individual's horizon. In Islam, for instance, the belief in the total sovereignty of God and in predestination can assist in dealing with trauma. The spiritual dimension of religion can furthermore play out productively in religious rituals that support processes of dealing with the past in a constructive manner. Giving structure and stability to daily life, rituals become even more significant in times of turmoil. Faith actors have used and creatively adapted religious rituals to open up pathways towards healing. In post-genocide Rwanda, for example, Catholic communities have modified the Christian sacrament of penance. The ritual of *gacaca nkirisitu* (Christian gacaca) guides genocide perpetrators and survivors in a structured manner towards reconciliation (Carney 2015).

Religion as Institution: Influencers on War and Peace

Religious leaders play a particularly important role in conflict and conflict transformation as they can exercise their influence over their followers for either end. Many people have seen the video clips of ISIS leaders in the Syrian civil war spreading hatred and invoking violence and destruction. At the same time, the course of history in post-apartheid South Africa was significantly shaped by religious leaders, such as Archbishop Desmond Tutu who led his fellow citizens on a path of peace and reconciliation rather than violent retaliation for decades of injustice and oppression. The institutional dimension of religion in peacebuilding also plays out in very practical ways in different forms of service delivery. Even in the midst of violent conflict, religious institutions oftentimes help to sustain minimum service infrastructure such as providing shelter, healthcare, and food. Being able to draw on their sometimes vast networks, religious institutions can mobilise additional human and financial resources for conflict transformation initiatives.

Religion as Framework: Holistic Human Flourishing

With its specific anthropology and understanding of human nature, religion offers a framework that can be used as a helpful resource in peacebuilding. With many secular actors focusing on the material, physical, and technical aspects of well-being, faith actors draw on a holistic concept of human flourishing that encompasses the physical, the spiritual, the material, and the emotional. This framework plays out in all stages of conflict transformation. In terms of conflict prevention, Laura Payne from the Centre for Trust, Peace and Social Relations at Coventry draws our attention to faith-based approaches "modelling forms of prevention embedded within local culture and that recognise the emotional and spiritual dimensions of transformative change" (Payne 2020: 1). The framework dimension of religion is also constructively employed in post-conflict settings. In post-genocide Rwanda, for example, reconciliation initiatives are oftentimes coupled with development projects. In the small town of Remera, the Presbyterian pastor and trained mediator initiated the "Lights", a group of volunteers dedicated to building relationships with and between genocide perpetrators and survivors. In weekly discussions, participants learn about Christian concepts such as forgiveness, transformation, and grace, and gain insights from trauma therapy, non-violent conflict resolution, and mediation. At the same time, pairs of perpetrators and survivors receive practical support, for instance, in the form of apple saplings. In the joint care of the saplings, relationships between former enemies can slowly grow, while the proceeds from the crops help to practically support their families. Welcome synergetic effects thus strengthen both the development and the reconciliation aspects of these initiatives, catering to both the spiritual-emotional and the physical dimensions of human nature.

Despite the fact that faith-based peacebuilding "still operates on the fringes of the larger field of peace and conflict resolution" (Abu-Nimer 2015: 16), it can bring potent resources to the field. At the same time, religious peacebuilding is also connected to potential problems and challenges that need to be mentioned at least briefly (cf. Schliesser et al. 2021). While proselytisation, and exacerbation of conflict are the two problems mentioned most often in this context, faith-based peacebuilding faces various additional challenges. These include the need for a better inclusion of youth and of women (Hayward & Marshall 2015), a deeper engagement with indigenous and non-Abrahamic faith traditions (Hayward 2012: 6–7), and the need for better evaluation. In the following spotlight from post-genocide Rwanda, Christophe Mbonyingabo illuminates the potentials and problems of faith-based peacebuilding and reconciliation in the aftermath of historical trauma from a Christian perspective.

Spotlight: A Christian Perspective on Reconciliation and Forgiveness After the Rwandan Genocide (Christophe Mbonyingabo)

Brief Background on the Genocide: What Happened?

During the colonial times, Rwanda was divided into three tribes, namely the Hutu, Tutsi, and Twa (or Batwa), with the aim to divide and rule the country. These three categories were previously fluid social classes based on the wealth of a person but were now transformed by the colonials into tribes. Since 1959, there was ongoing rivalry between the tribes, especially on the higher political level of the country. In 1994, Rwanda faced the worst of crimes against humanity: the genocide against the Tutsi. The roots of the genocide were in 1959, when the Hutus overthrew the Tutsi monarchy and tens of thousands of Tutsis fled to neighbouring countries. A group of Tutsi exiles formed a rebel group, the Rwandan Patriotic Front (RPF), which entered Rwanda in 1990 by force and fighting continued until a 1993 peace deal was agreed upon. The aim of the exile RPF was to return to their country. On April 6, 1994, a plane carrying the then-President Juvenal Habyarimana, and his Burundi counterpart, was shot down. Immediately after the plane crash, the killing of Tutsis started and in 100 days, over one million people were slaughtered by ethnic Hutu extremists. The genocide was eventually stopped by the RPF in July 1994.

Reconciliation in Rwanda After the Genocide

After the genocide against the Tutsi in 1994, the Rwandan government has been working on forming a strategic path for sustainable peace, unity, social cohesion, and socioeconomic development in Rwanda. Up to today, a lot has been done in line with reconciliation and rebuilding the country. Perpetrators have been tried and most of them have completed their sentences and are back in their villages. At the same time, survivors are being helped to heal and forgive those who persecuted their loved ones. Reconciliation is a road Rwanda started and will journey on for a long time, but its fruits are being seen today. The country is being restored and it is developing.

But forgiveness! How do you forgive after such atrocities? And the worst part is that your neighbours and your friends were the ones who were after you and destroyed your family! Forgiveness was not an easy word to mention in Rwanda after 1994, but it was the only hope for the country. However, daring as it was, after the genocide the country embarked on a journey of healing, forgiveness and reconciliation, and of rebuilding the infrastructures of the country. Different mechanisms were put in place to facilitate healing at the individual, community, and national levels. One of the best Rwandan instruments on this journey was the home-grown community-based courts called "Gacaca courts" that were institutionalised to bring to justice the genocide perpetrators. These were encouraged to confess their crimes and ask for forgiveness. The genocide survivors were also encouraged to forgive those who ask for forgiveness, and the perpetrators will come back to live together in the community. Today no one is referred to on the base of ethnicity, but rather "Ndumunyarwanda" (I am a Rwandan) is the identity promoted.

Today, Rwanda is one of the safest places in Africa, where crime rates are very low. According to the World Bank, economic growth in Rwanda averaged 7.2% over the decade to 2019, while per capita gross domestic product (GDP) grew at 5% annually. On July 14, 2021, the government put in place the ministry of

National Unity and Civic Engagement. The new ministry is to focus on national unity, preservation of historical memory, and promoting citizenship education.

Faith-Based Reconciliation Initiatives: The Example of CARSA

CARSA is a Rwandan local NGO that has a mission of serving communities in supporting their journey towards healing, forgiveness, reconciliation, and sustainable holistic development. Founded in 2002, CARSA's vision is to see a society where peace, solidarity and unity in diversity are being established. CARSA's programmes include, among others, trauma healing workshops, the Cows for Peace project, youth empowerment, and community development. Being a Christian FBO, it helps people to connect back with their faith as they connect with their neighbour.

Cows for Peace Intervention

Cows for Peace is a CARSA intervention developed in 2012 to promote sustainable reconciliation between genocidaires and survivors. This is achieved through three programmatic activities:

a. All participants complete a seven-day workshop focused on personal and relational changes. Multiple sessions are conducted with 36 identified genocidaire-survivor dyads. The workshop is adapted from a cognitive-behavioural-based programme designed to assist persons affected by war and conflict to acquire skills to cope with post-traumatic stressors and to support reconciliation efforts. For most participants, this is the first time that they have formally interacted with their direct perpetrator or victim in a structured group setting. This cognitive-behavioural-based group intervention contextualises Judeo-Christian themes of forgiveness and reconciliation, which are culturally fitting in Rwanda, a country with a vast Christian majority.
b. Reconciliation Cell Groups are self-led gatherings of genocidaire-survivor dyads who completed the workshops. They are hosted at local residential areas. These groups meet voluntarily and monthly under the direction of a group-appointed leader. The common aim is to foster sustained self-initiated interactions between dyads in a supportive group setting. Relationships between genocidaires and survivors that were established during the workshops continue to develop through discussions, communal meals, visitations, and joint activities (e.g. assistance with farming and home repairs). CARSA staff visit the groups to assist and support as needed in areas of navigating group conflict and clarification of group discussion topics.
c. The third programmatic activity is Cooperative Cow Raising by selected dyads of genocidaires and survivors. The historical and cultural significance of owning cattle in Rwanda creates a unique "superordinate goal" for genocidaire-survivor dyads to jointly work toward. Activities included

building a cow shed; purchasing feed for the cow; and washing, feeding, and grazing the cow. Milk, manure (for fertiliser), and income generated from the cow are shared between the two households. The cow is firstly raised on the survivor's property, and the calf to be conceived is given to the genocidaire.

This cow not only helps in bringing closer the people who are on the journey of reconciliation and their families, but it also contributes economically to poverty reduction of the pairs and fights against malnutrition with milk from the cow. It is very important that CARSA tackles those areas together because reconciliation, inner healing, and economic well-being do affect each other. The Cows for Peace project uniquely attends to all of these.

Role of the Christian Faith

At the time of the genocide, one of the most Christian nations in the region had become a home of blood and trauma. As Timothy Longman puts it, for some Rwandans the country's churches stand as reminders of the violence that decimated their families. The image of bodies piled at the altar does not easily fade from people's minds. Though statistics on the religious affiliations of people who have been accused were not collected, the religious demographics of Rwanda at the time mean that the vast majority of those people implicated in genocide were Christian.

Though the church was accused of playing a role in the genocide, still today 90% of the population claim to be Christians and the Christian faith continues to play an important role in the process of reconciliation. It is therefore important to ask the following question: Is faith relevant in reconciliation? In order to examine how reconciliation is practiced from a faith-based perspective in a predominantly Christian society, one must first understand the influence of church in the life of Rwandans in general.

Christian churches in Rwanda play an important role in shaping the Rwandan community, not only in religious matters but also with regard to social cohesion, and psychosocial and economic aspects. The churches' actions directly affect public perceptions (and utilisation of) communities of faith, and therefore its history is relevant to ways in which reconciliation is manifesting itself in Rwandan society today. The Christian faith is rooted in the forgiveness of sin and in reconciling God with humanity.

After the genocide, many church denominations developed programmes to address the issues of trauma healing, forgiveness, and reconciliation. The Catholic Church as the largest Christian denomination in Rwanda holds a place of great influence in Rwandese society. As a result, Catholic perceptions of forgiveness, reconciliation, atonement, and justice have influenced the way Rwandese public consciousness functions. Catholic views on forgiveness are shaped by Matthew 6, where Jesus states that God will forgive a person if he or she is able to forgive others. Furthermore, for Catholicism, confession of guilt is an essential part of the forgiveness and reconciliation process. The Pentecostal church then adds that reconciliation is an ongoing dedication of one's life to God, and this process may be interpreted in terms of forgiveness as well. Though the perpetrators are accepted into the community and forgiveness has been granted, the process of reconciliation of that perpetrator to God and to the survivors is a continuous process. While the destructive sides of religion surfaced in Rwanda before and during the genocide, the immense healing powers of the Christian faith also show themselves clearly now. The road to reconciliation and sustainable peace is still long, yet significant progress has been made.

12
NOW WHAT? IMPLICATIONS FOR ACADEMICS, POLICYMAKERS, AND PRACTITIONERS

About 85% of the people on this planet claim adherence to a faith (World Population Review 2022). Key development concepts such as equality, solidarity, education, or peace are at home in virtually all faith traditions. As much as the voices gathered in this book from around the globe differ in their specific faith traditions, their cultural and geographical backgrounds, they unanimously agree on one thing: Religion matters for the SDGs. From Pentecostal Christianity and its impact on poverty alleviation in South Africa to the contribution of Buddhism for quality education in Malaysia, to Muslim resources in opposing gender-based violence to the difference that multi-religious engagement makes in fighting the COVID-19 pandemic worldwide – religion plays a role, well, usually several roles. And there is one more thing that became clear: Religion is ambivalent. It can be used for good *and* for bad, for inciting violence and hatred *and* for bringing people together for reconciliation and peace. Religion is thus a powerful force that especially secular Western development discourse and practice has too long neglected.

So religion matters. Yet what does this mean concretely for academics, policymakers, and practitioners engaged in the development and the SDGs? Nine practical implications serve not only to close this book but much more importantly to open up further discussion and facilitate engagement to make this planet a better, more just and more peaceful home for ourselves and the generations to come. "The ultimate responsible question is not how I extricate myself heroically from a situation but [how] a coming generation is to go on living" (Bonhoeffer 2010, 42).

Implication 1: Beyond the Binary – Bridging the Religious-Secular Divide Effectively

"There is now indisputable and solid evidence that religions and religious actors can successfully be invited into, and contribute to global development. ... Thus,

DOI: 10.4324/9781003332275-15

there is a clear consensus that religious actors should be recognized and legitimized as important players in achieving the SDGs and other sustainability objectives" (Udenrigsministeriet 2019: 6). Despite the evidence cited by the Ministry of Foreign Affairs of Denmark, the cooperation of faith-based and secular development actors is still largely operating on the fringes of development discourse and practice. While no longer exactly exotic, faith-based and secular partnerships for the SDGs are still far from being mainstreamed. In order to effectively address suspicion, ignorance and uncertainties on all sides, much more remains to be done, including on the part of academics, policymakers, and practitioners. At the same time, religious engagement for the sake of religious engagement is not enough. Rather, "there must be a commitment to better religious engagement – real SRE [strategic religious engagement], … i.e. purposeful, self-aware, unrepetitive/duplicative" (Wilkinson 2021: 82). Religion matters for the SDGs – this sentence must become the premise for development theory and practice.

Implication 2: Reading Religion Right – Seven Dimensions of Religion

Yet work together with faith-based actors, there are many who have difficulties with recognising, analysing, and interpreting the oftentimes nebulous "religious factor" in an appropriate manner. Secular actors have repeatedly voiced the "ongoing need for shared analytical and definitional clarity when dealing with religion in development processes" (UNFPA 2014: 52). This difficulty is by no means distinct to secular actors alone, but many faith-based actors face the same challenge when asked to explain the uniqueness of their contributions. By introducing a seven-dimensional analytical model of religion, reading religion right becomes easier. In order to avoid misinterpreting religion through a simplistic lens, academics, policymakers, and practitioners benefit from being aware of the seven different faces of religion, namely, religion as religio-scape, community, teachings, spirituality, practice, institutions, and framework (cf. Chapter 5). Depending on each particular situation, some of these faces are more prominent than others. In conflict settings, for example, it might be the case that the dimensions of community, teachings, spirituality, and practice play a major role. Being aware of the potentials and the problems connected to these aspects can be tremendously helpful when trying to engage faith actors in the quest for peace and reconciliation.

Implication 3: Creating Spaces of Trust – The Need for Encounter Between All Relevant Actors

"Creating forums for interfaith and secular-religious debate on international development is an important step in understanding and respecting differences, as well as finding and pursuing shared goals" (SSRC 2011: 26). This recommendation resulting from a series of consultations on religion, development, and the

UN in 2011 has not lost any of its validity, nor urgency. Efforts in bridging the secular-faith binary need to be accompanied by bringing together the different spheres of engagement in development, namely policymakers, practitioners, and academics. Creating safe spaces for all relevant actors involved in development is crucial for trust building and information sharing. Policymakers and academics learn about the difficulties faced in the field, and practitioners can access valuable insights and suggest areas where more research is needed. Forums like the UN Inter-Agency Task Force (IATF) on Engaging with FBOs for Sustainable Development or the International Partnership on Religion and Sustainable Development (PaRD) provide these much-needed spaces of trust and should therefore be strengthened.

Implication 4: Bilinguality – Religious and Developmental Literacy

Academics, policymakers, and practitioners engaged in development work and discourse need to be bilingual, or rather, multilingual. Not only in the sense that "bad English is the new Latin" as the saying goes, but also in the sense that they need to develop skills in both religious and developmental literacy. On the one hand, secular actors need to increase their understanding of the different religious dimensions in social, political, or economic realities, and "learn their 'language' and culture" (UNFPA 2014: 51). Continuing education courses such as "Specialized Journalist Religion" for media professionals, offered by the Munich school for journalists ifp (ifp 2022), are but one helpful example of how religious literacy can be acquired. On the other hand, faith-based actors need to attain the competences to make themselves understandable to their non-faith-based counterparts. This often means familiarising oneself with human rights language. Bilinguality requires translation. Yet translation does not mean giving up your convictions but rather helping your partner from a different background to understand your perspective. While a faith-based actor, for example, would usually speak of the sacredness of humans in terms of being created in the image of God, in a pluralistic or secular development organisation she could choose the terminology of human dignity to make herself understandable. Working together effectively for the SDGs requires that we learn each other's languages. This necessitates investments in religious and development literacy.

Implication 5: Theology Matters – Why We Need Immanent Critics

Learning to speak the language of human rights is not enough for faith-based actors, however. The universal claim of human rights – as given shape by the SDGs – can only be realised if met by local integration. In other words: If human rights do not develop local roots, their universality erodes. It is thus the task of each and every single faith tradition to dig into their respective theologies in order to find interfaces with the concerns of human rights and the SDGs. Otherwise, there is the danger that human rights will be seen as something external, Western, and alien to one's own faith tradition. For this immensely important work, we need theologians who act as immanent critics, i.e. people who are intimately at home in their faith tradition, and who are willing to engage with it critically and self-critically. Coming from a problematic history herself, Christian theology, for example, is now slowly exploring the innate connection between human rights and its own core values of peace, justice, and solidarity. Sustainable development theory and practice thus need to support theologians, in all faith traditions, in their crucial work of acting as immanent critics and of finding overlaps between their own faith and the concern of human rights and the SDGs.

Implication 6: Women in Focus – Rethinking Religious Leadership

Clearly, religious leaders are fundamentally important for achieving sustainable social change. For this reason, multilateral outreach to faith actors in the development field oftentimes aims at religious leadership. Which, in turn, frequently means engaging older men. This, however, not only risks a gender-imbalanced representation of faith communities within development – which unwittingly counteracts SDG 5 on "Gender Equality" – but it also excludes the wisdom and experience of the very people engaged in practical development work on a day-to-day basis. "Either religious leadership has to be broadly (re)defined, or the very criteria for engagement of faith-based actors around the development policy tables has to change, to accommodate the voices and experiences of those who have the actual knowledge of serving girls', women's, children's and marginalized peoples' lives in almost every community around the world – i.e. women of faith" (UNFPA 2016: 37).

Implication 7: Youth in Focus – And What About Social Media?

In India, the use of social media has risen by more than 250% in the past seven years from 142 million users in 2015 to 370 million in 2022. The vast majority of users of social media platforms such as Facebook are between 13 and 34 years old (Singh Bhati & Bansal 2019). On the other side of the globe, we see a similar situation. In 2022, in 14 EU member states at least 9 out of 10 young people participate in social networking. With 69% of young people engaged in social media, France has the lowest numbers in the European Union (Eurostat 2022), while the other EU member states are somewhere between these figures. These numbers are in stark contrast to the representation of the SDGs on social media, however. Despite the fact that clearly social media is a highly effective tool to reach the youth, there is comparatively little engagement with youth on the intersection between faith and the SDGs via social media. During a collaborative meeting between faith-based and secular development organisations in 2015, "one organization shared that it could not find one organization in the Middle East that was working on issues of religion and peace through social media" (UNFPA 2016: 44). Needless to say, we must become better at utilising social media for reaching the youth on issues of faith and development.

Implication 8: What Good Is This? – Accountability and Measuring Impact

Dialogue and discussion between faith-based and secular development actors are good, but the dialogue and discussion leading to action is even better. Clear action plans that include guidelines and timelines for a variety of programmes improve accountability on all sides, which in turn allows trust to grow. Next to accountability, further challenges include impact and its measurement. Marshall et al. note that while "research and operational evaluations have expanded in recent years … there are, however, substantial gaps in evidence, most significantly regarding local and non-formal involvement" (Marshall et al. 2021: 42). In view of religious peacebuilding, a field that next to health is comparatively well documented, Mohammed Abu-Nimer and Renáta Katalin Nelson (eds. 2021: 1) point out, "The development of ethical and theoretical evaluation frameworks and procedures for religious and interreligious peacebuilding is not only an important step towards strengthening programmes and projects in the field, but also necessary for scholarly and professional recognition, as well as, communicating and engaging with policy-making circles and other agencies who influence the process of social change". One interesting example in this particular field is the Effective Interreligious Action in Peacebuilding framework, a collaborative effort in an evaluative design framework for both practitioners and evaluators (Garred et al. 2021). The methods and frameworks presented there could potentially be useful far beyond the realm of religious peacebuilding.

Implication 9: One Faith Is Not Enough – The Power of Multifaith Engagement

"Who is not at the table?" This question needs to inform all collaboration between faith-based and secular development actors. Even when faith-based actors have been included in discourse and practice, the focus is oftentimes on the Abrahamic religions – Judaism, Christianity, and Islam. This limited perspective excludes the wisdom and contributions of other faith traditions, such as indigenous and dharmic traditions. With their global reach, the SDGs depend on the joint effort of all affected, which includes people of all faith traditions. This entails a double challenge: one directed at secular development actors, and the other at different faith traditions. Firstly, secular development partners are called to broaden their horizons and include faith-based development partners beyond the Abrahamic traditions. At the same time, the different faith traditions are called to collaborate with each other, developing multi-religious narratives on the SDGs. One powerful example is the multifaith initiative Religions for Peace (RfP), the largest non-governmental multi-religious organisation. Six focal areas – peace and justice; gender equality; sustainable environment; freedom of thought, conscience, and religion; interreligious education; and multi-religious collaborations and partnerships – serve to address the world's pressing issues. Guided by the conviction that "ambitious goals and complex problems can best be tackled when different faith communities work together", RfP is a model par excellence that "interreligious work is not optional, but absolutely necessary" (RfP 2022).

REFERENCES

Abu-Nimer, Mohammed. (2015). "Religion and Peacebuilding: Reflections on Current Challenges and Future Prospects", *Journal of Interreligious Studies* 16: 14–29.

Abu-Nimer, Mohammed and Renáta Katalin Nelson (eds.). (2021). *Evaluating Interreligious Peacebuilding and Dialogue. Methods and Frameworks*. Berlin: De Gruyter.

Adams, Nathaniel. (2015). *Religion and Women's Empowerment in Bangladesh*, Berkley Center for Religion, Peace & World Affairs. Viewed from: https://berkleycenter.georgetown.edu/publications/religion-and-women-s-empowerment-in-bangladesh. [Date accessed: March 4, 2022].

Addae, Stephen. (1997). *The Evolution of Modern Medicine in a Developing Country: Ghana 1880-1960*. Edinburgh: Durham Academic Press.

Aga Khan Foundation. (2020). *About us*. Viewed from: www.akdn.org. [Date accessed: June 25, 2022].

Albert, Eleanor. (2018). *Christianity in China*. Council of Foreign Relations. Viewed from: https://www.cfr.org/backgrounder/christianity-china. [Date accessed: July 15, 2022].

Al-Khattab, H. (ed.) (2012). *English Translation of Musnad Imam Ahmad Bin Hanbal (5 vol set)*. Riyadh: Maktaba Dar-us-Salam.

All Triratna. (n.d.). *Buddhist action*. Viewed from: https://thebuddhistcentre.com/action/interreligious-climat-pilgrim-oslo. [Date accessed: July 2, 2022].

Anderson, Allan. (2001). "Pentecostals and Apartheid in South Africa during Ninety Years 1908-1998", *Cyberjournal for Pentecostal-Charismatic Research 9*. Viewed from: http://pctii.org/cyberj/cyberj9/anderson.html. [Date accessed: May 30, 2022].

Appleby, R. Scott. (1996). "Religion as an Agent of Conflict Transformation and Peacebuilding", in Chester A. Crocker, Fen O. Hampson and Pamela Aall (eds.), *Turbulent Peace: The Challenges of Managing International Conflict*. Washington, DC: USIP, 821–840.

Appleby, R. Scott. (2000). *The Ambivalence of the Sacred: Religion, Violence and Reconciliation*. Lanham, MD: Rowman & Littlefield Publishers.

Appleby, R. Scott. (2008). "Building Sustainable Peace: The Roles of Local and Transnational Religious Actors", in Thomas Banchoff (ed.), *Religious Pluralism, Globalization, and World Politics*. Oxford: Oxford University Press, 125–154.

Ardley, Jane. (2003). "Satyagraha in Tibet: Toward a Gandhian solution?" *The Tibet Journal* 28(4): 23–38.
Asadullah, M. Niaz, Sajeda Amin and Nazmul Chaudhury. (2019). "Support for Gender Stereotypes: Does Madrasah Education Matter?", *Journal of Development Studies* 55(1): 39–56.
Ashrof, V.A. Mohamad. (2005). *Islam and Gender Justice*. Delhi: Kalpaz Publications.
Ayedze, Kossi A. (2009). "Poverty Among African People and the Ambiguous Role of Christian Thought", in Peter J. Paris (ed.), *Religion and Poverty. Pan-African Perspectives*. Durham: Duke University Press, 193–212.
Babcock, Michael. (2016). *Susan Seddon Boulet. A Retrospective*. Portland, OR: Pomegranate.
Baerbock, Annalena. (2022). *Rede von Außenministerin Baerbock im Deutschen Bundestag am 29. September 2022: Aktuelle Stunde "Zu den Protesten im Iran nach dem Tod von Mahsa Amini in Polizeigewahrsam"*. Viewed from: https://www.auswaertiges-amt.de/de/newsroom/-/2555372. [Date accessed: October 30, 2022].
Bagir, Zainal A. and Najiyah Martiam. (2016). "Islam: Norms and Practices", in Willis J. Jenkins, Mary Evelyn Tucker and John Grim (eds.), *Routledge Handbook for Religion and Ecology*. London: Routledge, 79–87.
Balboni, M.J. and Balboni, T.A. (2019). *Hostility to Hospitality. Spirituality and Professional Socialization within Medicine*. New York, NY: Oxford University Press.
Barrett, William P. (2020). *America's Top 100 Charities*. Forbes. Viewed from: https://www.forbes.com/lists/top-charities/#176d86165f50. [Date accessed: May 30, 2022].
Bassous, Michael. (2015). "What are the Factors that Affect Worker Motivation in Faith Based Nonprofit Organizations?" *Voluntas: International Journal of Voluntary and Nonprofit Organizations* 26: 355–381. 10.1007/s11266-013-9420-3.
Bauer, Thomas. (2018). *Die Vereindeutigung der Welt. Über den Verlust an Mehrdeutigkeit und Vielfalt*. Stuttgart: Reclam.
Bedford-Strohm, Heinrich. (2009). "Politik und Religion – Öffentliche Theologie", *Verkündigung und Forschung* 54(2009): 42–55. 10.14315/vf-2009-54-2-42.
Ben-Gurion, David. (1948). *Declaration of Establishment of the State of Israel*. Viewed from: https://www.jewishvirtuallibrary.org/analysis-of-israel-s-declaration-of-establishment. [Date accessed: August 30, 2022].
Berger, Julia. (2003). "Religious Non-Governmental Organizations: An Exploratory Analysis", *Voluntas: International Journal of Voluntary and Nonprofit Organizations* 14(1): 15–39.
Berger, Peter L. (ed.). (1999). *The Desecularization of the World. Resurgent Religion and World Politics*. Grand Rapids, MI: Eerdmans.
Bessey, Sarah. (2013). *Jesus Feminist: An Invitation to Revisit the Bible's View of Women*. New York, NY: Howard Books.
Bonhoeffer, Dietrich. (2005). *Ethics*. Dietrich Bonhoeffer Works 6. Edited by Clifford Green. Minneapolis, MN: Fortress Press.
Bonhoeffer, Dietrich. (2010). *Letters and Papers from Prison*. Dietrich Bonhoeffer Works 8. Edited by John de Gruchy. Minneapolis, MN: Fortress Press.
Bouta, Tsjeard, S. Ayse Kadayifci-Orellana and Mohammed Abu-Nimer. (2005). *Faith-Based Peace-Building: Mapping and Analysis of Christian, Muslim, and Faith-Based Actors*. The Hague: Clingendael Institute.
Böckenförde, Ernst-Wolfgang. (1976). *Staat, Gesellschaft, Freiheit*. Frankfurt: Suhrkamp.
Buddhist Declaration on Climate Change. (2015). *The Time to Act is Now: A Buddhist Declaration on Climate Change*. May 14. Viewed from: https://fore.yale.edu/files/buddhist_climate_change_statement_5-14-15.pdf. [Date accessed: July 28, 2022].

Carland, Susan. (2017). *Islam and feminism are not mutually exclusive, and faith can be an important liberator*. The Conversation, 10 May. Viewed from: https://theconversation.com/islam-and-feminism-are-not-mutually-exclusive-and-faith-can-be-an-important-liberator-77086. [Date accessed: March 7, 2022].

Carlisle, Juliet E. and April K. Clark. (2018). "Green for God: Religion and Environmentalism by Cohort and Time", *Environment and Behavior* 50(2): 213–241.

Carney, Jay J. (2015). "A Generation After Genocide: Catholic Reconciliation in Rwanda", *Theological Studies* 76: 785–812.

Carson, Clayborne. (2013). *The Essential Martin Luther King, Jr. "I Have a Dream" and Other Great Writings*. Boston, MA: Beacon Press.

Chancel, Lucas, Piketty, Thomas, Saez, Emmanuel, Zucman, Gabriel et al., (2022). "World Inequality Report 2022". *World Inequality Lab*. Viewed from: https://wir2022.wid.world/. [Date accessed: May 12, 2022].

Chanda-Vaz, Urmi. (2020). *Can Religion Fight Climate Change?*, Mint, February 24. Viewed from: https://www.livemint.com/mint-lounge/features/can-religion-fight-climate-change-11582546478381.html. [Date accessed: July 28, 2022].

Chandra, Rayna. (2021). *The Decline of Democracy, Secularization, and Minority Rights in India*. Viewed from: https://berkleycenter.georgetown.edu/responses/the-decline-of-democracy-secularization-and-minority-rights-in-india. [Date accessed: June 23, 2022].

Christian Action for Reconciliation and Social Assistance (CARSA). (2022). *Welcome to CARSA*. Viewed from: www.carsaministry.org. [Date accessed: June 25, 2022].

Christian Solidarity International (CSI). (2017). *Hochgeschätzte Arbeit von Schwester Sara*. January 5, 2017. Viewed from: https://csi-schweiz.ch/artikel/hochgeschaetzte-arbeit-von-schwester-sara/. [Date accessed: September 1, 2022].

Cochrane, James R. and Gary R. Gunderson. (2012). *The Barefoot Guide to Mobilizing Religious Health Assets for Transformation*. Viewed from: www.barefoodguide.org. [Date accessed: July 31, 2022].

Coleman, Michael C. (2001). "'The Children Were Used Wretchedly': Pupil Responses to the Irish Charter Schools in the Nineteenth Century", *History of Education* 30: 339–357.

Communion of Protestant Churches in Europe (CPCE). (2021). *'Being church together in a pandemic' – Reflections from a Protestant Perspective*, CPCE focus 29. Viewed from: https://www.leuenberg.eu/cpce-content/uploads/2021/03/GEKE-focus-29-web.pdf. [Date accessed: July 31, 2022].

Council of the European Union. (2013). *EU Guidelines on the Promotion and Protection of Freedom of Religion or Belief*, Foreign Affairs Council meeting, Luxembourg, June 24, 1-18. Viewed from: https://eeas.europa.eu/sites/default/files/137585.pdf. [Date accessed: July 31, 2022].

Council on Biblical Manhood and Womanhood (CBMW). (1987). *The Danvers Statement*. Viewed from: http://www.girs.com/library/society/danversstatement.html. [Date accessed: March 4, 2022].

Dalli, Helena. (2020). *Corona-Krise: Frauen und Kinder brauchen jetzt mehr Schutz*. Frankfurter Rundschau May 11. Viewed from: https://www.fr.de/meinung/corona-krise-frauen-kinder-brauchen-mehr-schutz-13757365.html. [Date accessed: March 4, 2022].

Davis, Adam J. (2019). *The Medieval Economy of Salvation. Charity, Commerce, and the Rise of the Hospital*. New York, NY: Cornell University Press.

Davis, Comfort, Ayodele Jedgede, Robert Leurs, Adegbenga Sunmola and Ukoha Ukiwo. (2011). *Comparing Religious and Secular NGOs in Nigeria: Are Faith-Based Organizations Distinctive?*, Working Paper 56, Religion and Development Research Programme, International Development Department, University of Birmingham, UK.

de Gruchy, John and Charles Villa-Vicencio. (1983). *Apartheid is a Heresy.* Grand Rapids, MI: Eerdmans.

de Gruchy, John W. (2007). "Public Theology as Christian Witness. Exploring the Genre", *International Journal for Public Theology* 1(2007): 26–41.

De Waal, Alex. (2015). "Armed Conflict and the Challenge of Hunger: Is an End in Sight?", Global Hunger Index 2015, 23. Viewed from: http://www.welthungerhilfe.de/en/globalhungerindex2015.html. [Date accessed: August 27, 2022].

Dickow, Helga. (2012). *Religion and Attitudes towards Life in South Africa: Pentecostals, Charismatics, and Reborns.* Baden-Baden: Nomos.

Durkheim, Émile. (1915). *The Elementary Forms of Religious Life* (trans. by J.W. Swain). London: Allen & Unwin.

Encyclopaedia Britannica. (2000). *Syria.* Viewed from: https://www.britannica.com/place/Syria/The-winds. [Date accessed: May 31, 2022].

Epstein-Peterson, Zachary D., Adam J. Sullivan, Andrea C. Enzinger, Kelly Trevino, Angelika A. Zollfrank, Michael Balboni, Tyler J. VanderWeele and Tracy A. Balboni. (2015). "Examining Forms of Spiritual Care Provided in the Advanced Cancer Setting", *American Journal of Hospice and Palliative Medicine* 32: 750–757. 10.1177/1049909114540318.

Erikson, Erik H. (1968). *Identity: Youth and crisis.* New York, NY: Norton.

Eurostat. (2022). *Being young in Europe today – digital.* Viewed from: https://ec.europa.eu/eurostat/statistics-explained/index.php?title=Being_young_in_-Europe_today_-_digital_world#Youth_online:_a_way_of_life. [Date accessed: June 20, 2022].

Folarin, George O. (2007). "Contemporary State of the Prosperity Gospel in Nigeria", *The Asia Journal of Theology* 21(1): 69–95.

Frahm-Arp, Maria. (2018). "Pentecostalism, Politics, and Prosperity in South Africa", *Religions* 9(10): 298. 10.3390/rel9100298.

Francis, Pope. (2015). *Laudato Sí: On Care for Our Common Home.* Vatican City: Our Sunday Visitor Publishing Division.

Frazer, Owen and Richard Friedli. (2015). *Approaching Religion in Conflict Transformation: Concepts, Cases and Practical Implications,* Center for Security Studies (CSS), ETH Zurich. Viewed from: www.css.ethz.ch/content/dam/ethz/special-interest/gess/cis/center-for-securities-studies/pdfs/Approaching-Religion-In-Conflict-Transformation2.pdf. [Date accessed: May 30, 2022].

Frazer, Owen and Mark Owen. (2018). *Religion in Conflict and Peacebuilding: Analysis Guide.* Washington, DC: United States Institute of Peace. Viewed from https://www.usip.org/programs/religious-peacebuilding-action-guides. [Date accessed: September 8, 2022].

Freeman, Dena. (2012). "The Pentecostal Ethic and the Spirit of Development", in Dena Freeman (ed.), *Pentecostalism and Development. Churches, NGOs and Social Change in Africa.* New York, NY: Palgrave Macmillan, 1–38.

Freeman, Dena. (2020). "Mobilising Evangelicals for Development Advocacy: Politics and Theology in the Micah Challenge Campaign for the Millennium Development Goals", in Jens Koehrsen and Andreas Heuser (eds.), *Faith-Based Organizations in Development Discourses and Practice.* New York and London: Routledge, 57–85.

Gallego, Francisco and Robert Woodberry. (2008). "Christian Missionaries and Education in Former Colonies: How Institutions Mattered", *Documento de Trabajo* 339, Santiago de Chile: Instituto de Economia. Pontificia Universidad Catolica de Chile.

Galtung, Johan. (1990). "Cultural Violence", *Journal of Peace Research* 27(3): 291–305.

Garred, Michelle, Elizabeth Hume and Rebecca Herrington. (2021). Linking "Evaluators and Inter-Religious Peacebuilders. The Making of an Evaluation Guide", in Mohammed

Abu-Nimer and Renáta Katalin Nelson (eds.), *Evaluating Interreligious Peacebuilding and Dialogue. Methods and Frameworks*. Berlin: De Gruyter, 169–195.

Georgetown University. Berkley Center for Religion, Peace & World Affairs. (2013). *A Discussion with Edna Adan Ismail, Director and Founder of the Edna Adan Maternity Hospital in Hargeisa, Somaliland*. Viewed from: https://berkleycenter.georgetown.edu/interviews/a-discussion-with-edna-adan-ismail-director-and-founder-of-the-edna-adan-maternity-hospital-in-hargeisa-somaliland. [Date accessed: July 31, 2022].

Gifford, Paul. (2016). *Christianity, Development, and Modernity in Africa*. New York, NY: Oxford University Press.

Gilliat-Ray, Sophie and Mark Bryant. (2011). "Are British Muslims 'Green'? An Overview of environmental activism among Muslims in Britain", *Journal for the Study of Religion, Nature & Culture* 5(3): 284–306. 10.1558/jsrnc.v5i3.284.

Girls Not Brides. (2022). *Power to girls*. Viewed from: www.girlsnotbrides.org. [Date accessed: June 25, 2022].

Giving USA Foundation. (2020). *Giving USA 2020: The Annual Report on Philanthropy for the Year 2019*. Viewed from: https://givingusa.org/. [Date accessed: May 30, 2022].

Gopin, Marc. (2009). *To Make the Earth Whole: The Art of Citizen Diplomacy in an Age of Religious Militancy*. Lanham, MD: Roman & Littlefield.

Gottschall, Jonathan. (2013). *The Storytelling Animal: How Stories Make Us Human*. Boston, MA: Mariner Books.

Grace, Gerald R. and Joseph O'Keefe (eds.). (2007). *International Handbook of Catholic Education: Challenges for School Systems in the 21st Century*. Dordrecht: Springer.

Granovetter, Marc. (1973). "The Strength of Weak Ties", *American Journal of Sociology*, 78(1): 1360–1380.

GreenFaith. (n.d.). *Greenfaith*. Viewed from: https://greenfaith.org/. [Date accessed: July 9, 2022].

Göçmen, İpek. (2013). "The Role of Faith-Based Organizations in Social Welfare Systems: A comparison of France, Germany, Sweden, and the United Kingdom", *Nonprofit and Voluntary Sector Quarterly* 42(3): 495–516. 10.1177/0899764013482046.

Hackett, Conrad and David McClendon. (2017). *Christians remain world's largest religious group, but they are declining in Europe*. Pew Research Center. Viewed from: https://www.pewresearch.org/fact-tank/2017/04/05/christians-remain-worlds-largest-religious-group-but-they-are-declining-in-europe/. [Date accessed: July 5, 2022].

Harpviken, Kristian Berg and Hanne Eggen Røislien. (2005). *Mapping the Terrain. The Role of Religion in Peacemaking*. State of the Art Paper to the Norwegian Ministry of Foreign Affairs. Oslo: PRIO.

Hasu, Päivi. (2012). "Prosperity Gospels and Enchanted Worldviews: Two Responses to Socio-economic Transformation in Tanzanian Pentecostal Christianity", in Dena Freeman (ed.), *Pentecostalism and Development. Churches, NGOs and Social Change in Africa*. London: Palgrave Macmillan, 67–86.

Haustein, Jörg and Emma Tomalin. (2019). *Keeping Faith in 2030: Religions and the Sustainable Development Goals. Findings and Recommendations*. Viewed from: https://religions-and-development.leeds.ac.uk/research-network/. [Date accessed: July 31, 2022].

Haynes, Jeffrey. (2007). *Religion and Development. Conflict or Cooperation?* New York, NY: Palgrave Macmillan.

Haynes, Jeffrey. (2020). "World Vision and 'Christian values' at the United Nations", in Jens Koehrsen and Andreas Heuser (eds.), *Faith-Based Organizations in Development Discourses and Practice*. New York and London: Routledge, 86–112.

Hayward, Susan. (2012). *Religion and Peacebuilding. Reflections on Current Challenges and Future Prospects*. USIP Special Report. Washington, DC: USIP. Viewed from: https://www.usip.org/publications/2012/08/religion-and-peacebuilding. [Date accessed: July 31, 2022].

Hayward, Susan and Katherine Marshall. (2015). *Women, Religion and Peacebuilding. Illuminating the Unseen*. Washington, DC: USIP.

Heist, Dan and Ram A. Cnaan. (2016). "Faith-Based International Development Work: A Review", *Religions* 7(19): 1–17.

Hekmatpour, Peyman. (2020). "Right-Wing Stewards: The Promoting Effect of Religiosity on Environmental Concern among Political Conservatives in a Global Context", *Social Problems* spaa066: 1–26. 10.1093/socpro/spaa066.

Heuser, Andreas. (2013). "'Refuse to Die in Poverty!' Armutsüberwindung und Varianten des Wohlstandsevangeliums in Afrika", *Theologische Zeitschrift* 69: 146–171.

Heuser, Andreas (ed.). (2015). *Pastures of Plenty: Tracing Religio-Scapes of Prosperity Gospel in Africa and Beyond*. Frankfurt: Peter Lang.

Holman, Susan R. (2015). *Beholden. Religion, Global Health, and Human Rights*. New York, NY: Oxford University Press.

Honderich, Holly. (2021). "Why Canada is mourning the deaths of hundreds of children", *BBC News*, 15 July. Viewed from: https://www.bbc.com/news/world-us-canada-57325653. [Date accessed: August 25, 2022].

Hoverd, William J. and Chris G. Sibley. (2013). "Religion, Deprivation and Subjective Wellbeing: Testing a Religious Buffering Hypothesis", *International Journal of Wellbeing* 3(2): 182–196. 10.5502/ijw.v3i2.5.

Howard, Brian. (2020). *Religion in Africa: Tolerance and Trust in Leaders Are High, But Many Would Allow Regulation of Religious Speech*. Afrobarometer Dispatch 339. Viewed from: https://afrobarometer.org/sites/default/files/publications/Policy%20papers/ab_r7_dispatchno339_pap12_religion_in_africa.pdf. [Date accessed: May 30, 2022].

Huber, Wolfgang. (1996). *Gerechtigkeit und Recht. Grundlinien christlicher Rechtsethik*. Gütersloh: Gütersloher Verlagshaus.

Hurma Project. (2019). *Upholding the sacred inviolability of all who enter Muslim spaces from exploitation & abuse by those holding religious power & authority*. Viewed from: https://hurmaproject.com. [Date accessed: July 2, 2022].

Ifp (Die katholische Journalistenschule). (2022). *Fachjournalist/in Religion*. Viewed from: https://journalistenschule-ifp.de/seminardetails/1037. [Date accessed: August 31, 2022].

International Commission on Financing Global Education Opportunity (Education Commission). (2016). *The Learning Generation: Investing in Education for a Changing World*. Viewed from: https://report.educationcommission.org/report/. [Date accessed: June 30, 2022].

International Committee of the Red Cross (ICRC). (2021). *You Are Not Alone: The Movement's Response to the COVID-19 Pandemic in Bosnia-Herzegovina*. Viewed from: https://www.icrc.org/en/document/red-cross-covid-19-response-bosnia-herzegovina/ [Date accessed: May 30, 2022].

International Partnership on Religion and Sustainable Development (PaRD). (n.d.). *About. Partnership Principles*. Viewed from: https://www.partner-religion-development.org/about/partnership-principles. [Date accessed: August 5, 2022].

International Partnership on Religion and Sustainable Development (PaRD). (2016). *Voices from Religions on Sustainable Development*. German Ministry for Economic Cooperation and Development (BMZ). Viewed from: https://www.partner-religion-development.

org/fileadmin/Dateien/Resources/Knowledge_Center-/Voices_from_Religions_on_Sustainable_Development_April2017_3rd_edition.pdf. [Date accessed: August 28, 2022].

International Society for Krishna Consciousness (ISKCON). (2021). *Education*. Viewed from: https://www.iskcon.org/activities/education.php. [Date accessed: July 31, 2022].

Islamic Relief. (2019). *An Islamic human rights perspective on early and forced marriage. Protecting the sanctity of marriage*. Viewed from: https://islamic-relief.org.my/wp-content/uploads/2019/02/human-rights-perspective-on-efm.pdf. [Date accessed: March 4, 2022].

Israel Central Bureau of Statistics (ICBS). (2020). *Population of Israel on the Eve of 2021*. Viewed from: https://www.cbs.gov.il/en/mediarelease/Pages/2020/-Population-of-Israel-on-the-Eve-of-2021.aspx. [Date accessed: August 28, 2022].

Ikeda, Daisaku. (2004). *Light of Education: Thoughts and Vision for Humanistic Education. Thoughts on the Aims of Education*. Kuala Lumpur: Soka Gakkai Malaysia.

Jahangir, Asma. (2000). "Human Rights in Pakistan: A System in the Making", in Samantha Power and Graham Allison (eds.), *Realizing Human Rights: Moving from Inspiration to Impact*. New York, NY: St Martin Press, 167–194.

Johnson, Lauren and Barbra Mann Wall. (2014). "Women, Religion, and Maternal Health Care in Ghana, 1945-2000", *Family & Community Health* 37: 223–230.

Joint Learning Initiative on Faith & Local Communities (JLI). (2022). *The State of Evidence in Religions and Development*. Washington, DC: JLI. https://jliflc.com/resources/the-state-of-the-evidence-in-religions-and-development/. [Date accessed: October 30, 2022].

Jones, Ben. (2012). "Pentecostalism, Development NGOs and Meaning", in Dena Freeman (ed.), *Pentecostalism and Development: Churches, NGOs and Social Change in Africa*. London: Palgrave Macmillan, 181–202.

Jungfreisinnige. (2020). *Medienmitteilungen*. Viewed from: https://jungfreisinnige.ch/stimmrechtsbeschwerden-in-vier-kantonen-kirchliches-engagement-fuer-die-sog-konzernverantwortungsinitiative-ist-bundesverfassungswidrig/. [Date accessed: May 30, 2022].

Kagawa, Rose C., Andrew Anglemyer and Dominic Montagu. (2012). "The Scale of Faith Based Organization Participation in Health Service Delivery in Developing Countries: Systematic Review and Meta-Analysis", *PLoS ONE* 7(11): e48457. 10.1371/journal.pone.0048457.

Keating, Frank. (2013). *In the United States, 50 percent of social services are provided by the Catholic church*. Politifact March 17. Viewed from: https://www.politifact.com/factchecks/2013/mar/19/frank-keating/does-catholic-church-provide-half-social-services-/. [Date accessed: January 7, 2022].

Keister, Lisa A. (2011). *Faith and Money: How Religion Contributes to Wealth and Poverty*. New York, NY: Cambridge University Press.

Khalaf-Elledge, Nora. (2020). "It's a Tricky One" – Development Practitioners' Attitudes Towards Religion", *Development in Practice*, 1–12. 10.1080/09614524.2020.1760210.

Kimball, Charles. (2002). *When Religion Becomes Evil*. San Francisco, CA: HarperCollins.

King, Martin Luther Jr. (1986). "Pilgrimage to Nonviolence", in James Melvin Washington (ed.), *A Testament of Hope: The Essential Writings and Speeches of Martin Luther King Jr*. San Francisco, CA: HarperCollins, 35–40.

King, Pamela E. (2003). "Religion and Identity: The Role of Ideological, Social, and Spiritual Contexts", *Applied Development Science* 7(3): 197–204. 10.1207/S15324 80XADS0703_11.

Klemm, Johannes. (2021). *Die Kirchen Treten Selbstbewusster Auf"*, Interview with Johannes Klemm, *reformiert* March 09. Viewed from: https://reformiert.info/de/recherche/

ldie-kirchen-muessen-diplomatischer-agieren-aber-sie-treten-selbstbewusster-aufr-19554.html. [Date accessed: May 30, 2022].

Knesset. (1992). *Basic Law: Human Dignity and Liberty*. Viewed from: https://www.mfa.gov.il/mfa/mfa-archive/1992/pages/basic%20law-%20human%20dignity%20and%20liberty-.aspx. [Date accessed: August 31, 2022].

Koehrsen, Jens. (2021). "Muslim and Climate Change. How Islam Muslim organizations, And Religious Leaders Influence Climate Change Perceptions and Mitigation Activities", *WIREs Climate Change* 12: e702. 10.1002/wcc.702.

Koehrsen, Jens and Andreas Heuser. (2020). "Beyond Established Boundaries: FBOs as developmental entrepreneurs", in Jens Koehrsen and Andreas Heuser (eds.), *Faith-Based Organizations in Development Discourses and Practice*. New York and London: Routledge, 1–29.

Koenig, Harold G. (2012). "Religion, Spirituality, and Health: The Research and Clinical Implications", *ISRN Psychiatry* 2012: 1–33. 10.5402/2012/278730.

Koenig, Harold G., Dana E. King and Verna B. Carson. (2012). *Handbook of Religion and Health* (2nd ed.). New York, NY: Oxford University Press.

Krause, Cornelia. (2021). "Kirche hat eine Schlüsselrolle im Kampf gegen das Virus", *Reformiert* 6: 1.

Kruglanski, Arie W., Xiaoyan Chen, Mark Dechesne, Shira Fishman and Edward Orehek. (2009). "Fully Committed: Suicide Bombers' Motivation and the Quest for Personal Significance", *Political Psychology* 30: 341–344. 10.1111/j.1467-9221.2009.00698.x.

Kusrin, Zuliza M., Zaini Nasohah, Mohd al-Adib Samuri and Mat Noor Mat Zain. (2013) "Legal Provisions and Restrictions on the Propagation of Non-Islamic Religions Among Muslims in Malaysia", *Kajian Malaysia* 31(2), 1–18.

Lama, Dalai. (1992). *A Buddhist Concept of Nature*. His Holiness, the 14th Dalai Lama of Tibet. Transcript of an address on February 4, 1992, at New Delhi, India. Viewed from: https://www.dalailama.com/messages/environment/buddhist-concept-of-nature. [Date accessed: July 28, 2022].

LeVine, Robert A., Sarah LeVine, Beatrice Schnell-Anzola, Meredith L. Rowe and Emily Dexter. (2012). *Literacy and Mothering: How Women's Schooling Changes the Lives of the World's Children*. New York, NY: Oxford University Press.

Lindbeck, George. (1984). *The Nature of Doctrine: Religion and Theology in a Postliberal Age*. Philadelphia, PA: Westminster Press.

Long, Norman. (2012). "Foreword", in Dena Freeman (ed.), *Pentecostalism and Development. Churches, NGOs and Social Change in Africa*. London: Palgrave Macmillan, vii–x.

Lotasaruaki, S. Loilang'isho. (2006). *Si mapenzi ya Mungu tuwe maskini*. Arusha.

Luther, Martin. (1959). *Book of Concord*. (edited and translated by Theodore G. Tappert). Philadelphia, PA: Fortress Press.

Magis Americas. (n.d.). *Education*. Viewed from: https://www.magisamericas.org/our-work/education/. [Date accessed: June 25, 2022].

Mandela, Nelson. (1998). *Together on the Way. Address by President Nelson Mandela to the WCC on the Occasion of its 50th Anniversary*, Harare, Zimbabwe, 13 December.

Marshall, Katherine. (2018). "Global education Challenges: Exploring Religious Dimensions", *International Journal of Educational Development* 62: 184–191.

Marshall, Katherine. (2020). What Religion Can Offer in the Response to COVID-19. Viewed from: https://www.worldpoliticsreview.com/insights/28789/religion-and-covid-19-faith-during-a-pandemic. [Date accessed: July 31, 2022].

Marshall, Katherine and Richard Marsh. (2003). *Millennium Challenges for Faith and Development Leaders*. Washington, DC: World Bank.

Marshall, Katherine and Marisa Van Saanen. (2007). *Development and Faith: Where Mind, Heart, and Soul Work Together*. Washington, DC: World Bank Publications.

Marshall, Katherine, Sudipta Roy, Chris Seiple and Hugo Slim. (2021). "Religious Engagement in Development: What Impact Does it Have?", *The Review of Faith & International Affairs* 19(sup1): 42–62, 10.1080/15570274.2021.1983347.

Marshall, Ruth. (1992). "Pentecostalism in Southern Nigeria", in Paul Gifford (ed.), *New Dimensions in African Christianity*. Ibada: Sefer, 8–39.

Marthoz, Jean-Paul and Joseph Saunders. (2005). *Religion and the Human Rights Movement*. Viewed from: https://www.hrw.org/legacy/wr2k5/religion/1.htm. [Date accessed: August 25, 2022].

Mathole, Ezekiel M.K. (2008). "Beyond Common Stereotypes about the Pentecostal-Charismatic Evangelicals in South Africa", in Helga Dickow and Andreas Heuser (eds.), *Religion on the Move: Exploring Passages in South African Christianity*. Beirut: Byblos, 59–75.

Maxwell, Melody. (2021). *Where Are the Women in American Evangelicalism?* Viewed from: https://berkleycenter.georgetown.edu/responses/where-are-the-women-in-american-evangelicalism The Future of U.S. Evangelical Christianity. [Date accessed: March 4, 2022].

McDonagh, Philip. (2019). *Religion and Security-Building in the OSCE-Context. Involving Religious Leaders and Congregations in Joint Efforts*. OSCE Network. Viewed from: https://osce-network.net/fileadmin/user_upload/publications/Religion_and_Security-Building_in_the_OSCE_Context_final.pdf. [Date accessed: July 5, 2022].

Mir-Hosseini, Ziba, Mulki Al-Sharmani and Jana Rumminger. (2015). *Men in Charge? Rethinking Authority in Muslim Legal Tradition*. London: Oneworld Publications.

Mombo, Esther M. (2009). "Religion and Materiality. The Case of Poverty Alleviation", in Peter J. Paris (ed.). *Religion and Poverty. Pan-African Perspectives*. Durham: Duke University Press, 213–227.

Moore, Diane L. (2016). "Diminishing Religious Literacy: Methodological Assumptions and Analytical Frameworks for Promoting the Public Understanding of Religion", in Adam Dinham and Matthew Francis (eds.), *Religious Literacy in Policy and Practice*. Bristol: Policy Press, 27–38.

Mueller, Paul S., David J. Plevak and Teresa Rummans. (2001). "Religious Involvement, Spirituality, and Medicine: Implications for Clinical Practice", *Mayo Clinic Proceedings* 76: 1225–1235.

Mwiria, K. (1991). "Education for Subordination: African Education in Colonial Kenya", *History of Education* 20: 261–273.

Nasr, Seyyed Hossein. (1997). *Man and Nature: The Spiritual Crisis in Modern Man*. Chicago: Kazi Publishers.

Nita, Maria. (2014). "Christian and Muslim Climate Activists Fasting and Praying for the Planet: Emotional Translation Of 'Dark Green' Activism and Green Faith Identities", in Robin G. Veldman, Andrew Szasz and Randolph Haluza-DeLay (eds.), *How the World's Religions are Responding to Climate Change: Social Scientific Investigations*. London: Routledge, 229–243.

Olivier, Jill, Clarence Tsimpo, Regina Gemignani, Mari Shojo, Harold Coulombe, Frank Dimmock, Minh C. Nguyen, Harrison Hines, Edward J. Mills, Joseph L. Dieleman, Annie Haakenstad and Quentin Wodon. (2015). "Understanding the Roles of Faith-Based Health-Care Providers in Africa: Review of the Evidence with a Focus on Magnitude, Reach, Cost, and Satisfaction", *Lancet* 386: 1765–1775. 10.1016/S0140-6736(15)60251-3.

Oxfam International. (2020). *Time to Care: Unpaid and Underpaid Care Work and the Global Inequality Crisis.* Viewed from: https://ousweb-prodv2-shared-media.s3.amazonaws.com/media/documents/FINAL_bp-time-to-care-inequality-200120-en.pdf. [Date accessed: September 20, 2022].

Palik, Júlia, Anna Marie Obermeier and Siri Aas Rustad. (2022). *Conflict Trends: A Global Overview, 1946-2021.* Oslo: PRIO. Viewed from https://reliefweb.int/report/world/conflict-trends-global-overview-1946-2021. [Date accessed: October 5, 2022].

Payne, Laura. (2020). "What Can Faith-Based Forms of Violent Conflict Prevention Teach Us About Liberal Peace?", *Religions* 11(4): 167. 10.3390/rel11040167.

Perchoc, Philippe. (2016). *Religious Organisations and Conflict Resolution.* Briefing. European Parliamentary Research Service, 1–8. Viewed from: https://www.europarl.europa.eu/thinktank/en/document.html?reference=EPRS_BRI(2016)593515. [Date accessed: July 31, 2022].

Pertek, Sandra. (2022). *Religion, Forced Migration and the Continuum of Violence: An Intersectional and Ecological Analysis.* PhD Thesis. University of Birmingham.

Pew Research Center. (2015). *The Future of World Religions: Population Growth Projections, 2010-2050.* Viewed from: https://www.pewresearch.org/religion/2015/04/02/religious-projections-2010-2050/. [Date accessed: August 8, 2022].

Pew Research Center. (2017). *The Changing Global Religious Landscape.* Viewed from: https://www.pewresearch.org/religion/2017/04/05/the-changing-global-religious-landscape/. [Date accessed: September 10, 2022].

Prothero, Stephen. (2008). *Religious Literacy: What every American Needs to Know About Religion (and Doesn't).* New York, NY: HarperOne.

Pullella, Philip. (2020). *Vatican Releases Financial Figures, Promises Transparency.* Reuters.com, October 1. Viewed from: https://www.reuters.com/article/us-vatican-finances-idUSKBN26M5XD. [Date accessed: September 10, 2022].

Qur'an. (2013). Translated by Abdullah Yusuf Ali. Ware, Hertfordshire: Wordsworth Editions Limited.

Raftery, Deirdre. (2012). "Religions and the History of Education: A Historiography", *History of Education* 41: 41–56. 10.1080/0046760X.2011.640355.

Raihhelgauz, Rebeka Mia. (2022). "ÜHISOSA" – Miks Me Seda Varem Ei Ole Teinud?", Teekäija Kristlik Ajakiri AAstttast 1904. Viewed from: https://teek.ee/teemad/37-noored/2922-uehisosa-miks-me-seda-varem-ei-ole-teinud. [Date accessed: 8 August 2022].

Rakodi, Carole. (2015). "Development, Religion and Modernity", in Emma Tomalin (ed.), *The Routledge Handbook of Religions and Global Development.* London and New York: Routledge, 17–35.

Rawls, John. (1993). *Political Liberalism* (Expanded Edition). New York, NY: Columbia University Press.

Religion Media Centre (RMC). (2022). *Religion Media Centre.* Viewed from: https://religionmediacentre.org.uk/. [Date accessed: July 8, 2022].

Religions for Peace (RfP). (2022). *Our Goal.* Viewed from: https://www.rfp.org/. [Date accessed: July 20, 2022].

Renquin, Jules (1921). *Les Devoirs des Missionnaires Dans Notre Colonie. Avenir Colonial Belge.* Brussels, 30 October.

Roberts, Nicole F. (2019). "Science Says: Religion is Good for Your Health", Forbes, March 29. Viewed from: https://www.forbes.com/sites/nicolefisher-/2019/03/29/science-says-religion-is-good-for-your-health/. [Date accessed: July 31, 2022].

Roy, Sudipta, Samia Huq and Aisha Binte Abdur Rob. (2020). "Faith and Education in Bangladesh: A Review of the Contemporary Landscape and Challenges", *International Journal of Educational Development* 79: 1–19. 10.1016/j.ijedudev.2020.102290

Schliesser, Christine. (2014). "On a Long Neglected Player: The Religious Dimension in Poverty Alleviation. The Example of the So-Called Prosperity Gospel in Africa", *Exchange* 43: 339–359.

Schliesser, Christine. (2018). "The Politics of Reconciliation", in Martin Leiner and Christine Schliesser (eds.), *Alternative Approaches in Conflict Resolution*. Basingstoke: Palgrave Macmillan, 137–146.

Schliesser, Christine. (2020). "Conflict Resolution and Peacebuilding", in Jeffrey Haynes (ed.), *Routledge Handbook of Religion and Political Parties*. London: Routledge, 126–138.

Schliesser, Christine. (2021). "Menschenrechte – Zum Beitrag theologischer Ethik im aktuellen Menschenrechtsdiskurs", *Zeitschrift für evangelische Ethik* 65: 261–272.

Schliesser, Christine, Ayse Kadayifci-Orellana and Pauline Kollontai. (2021). *Religion Matters – On the Significance of Religion in Conflict and Conflict Resolution*. London: Routledge Press. Viewed from: https://www.routledge.com/On-the-Significance-of-Religion-in-Conflict-and-Conflict-Resolution/Schliesser-Kadayifci-Orellana-Kollontai/p/book/9780367433925. [Date accessed: May 30, 2022].

Schweiger, Gottfried. (2019). "Religion and Poverty", *Palgrave Communications*, 5(59): 1–3. 10.1057/s41599-019-0272-3.

Seiple, Chris, Katherine Marshall, Hugo Slim and Sudipta Roy. (2021). "Strategic Religious Engagement in International Development: Building a Basic Baseline," *The Review of Faith & International Affairs* 19(sup1): 1–11, 10.1080/15570274.2021.1983360.

Sherwood, Harriet. (2018). *Religion: Why Faith is Becoming More and More Popular*. The Guardian, August 27. Viewed from: https://www.theguardian.com/news/2018/aug/27/religion-why-is-faith-growing-and-what-happens-next. [Date accessed: July 2, 2022].

Sider, Ron and Heidi R. Unruh. (2004). "Typology of Religious Characteristics of Social Service and Educational Organizations and Programs", *Nonprofit and Voluntary Sector Quarterly* 33(1): 109–134.

Silver, Harold. (1992). "Knowing and Not Knowing in the History of Education", *History of Education* 21: 97–108.

Singh Bhati, Vikramaditya and Jayshri Bansal. (2019). "Social Media and Indian Youth", *International Journal of Computer Sciences and Engineering* 7: 818–821.

Sloan, David. (2020). "American Evangelicals and the Resistance to the COVID Vaccines", *Deutsche Welle*, December 16. Viewed from: https://www.dw.com/en/american-evangelicals-and-the-resistance-to-covid-vaccines/a-55957915. [Date accessed: July 31, 2022].

Smyre, Christopher L., Hyo Jung Tak, Augustine P. Dang, Farr A. Curlin and John D. Yoon. (2018). "Physicians' Opinions on Engaging Patients' Religious and Spiritual Concerns: A National Survey", *Journal of Pain and Symptom Management* 55: 897–905.

Social Science Research Council (SSRC). (2012). *Religion, Development and the United Nations*. Edited by Azza Karam. New York: Social Science Research Council.

Southern Baptist Convention (SBC). (2022). *Baptist Faith & Message 2000*. Viewed from: https://bfm.sbc.net/bfm2000/. [Date accessed: March 7, 2022].

Staff, Toi. (2020). "Jerusalem Court Nixes Greek Church Bid to Stop Property Sale to Right Wing Group". *Times of Israel*. June 25. Viewed from: https://www.timesofisrael.com/jerusalem-court-nixes-greek-church-bid-to-stop-property-sale-to-right-wing-group/. [Date accessed: August 31, 2022].

Statista. (2021). *Global Military Spending From 2001 to 2020*. Viewed from: https://www.statista.com/statistics/264434/trend-of-global-military-spending/. [Date accessed: July 5, 2022].
Statistics South Africa (StatsSA). (2017a). *Living Conditions Survey 2014-2015*. Pretoria: Statistics South Africa. 10.258828/9229-xz60.
Statistics South Africa (StatsSA). (2017b). *Poverty Trends in South Africa. An Examination of Absolute Poverty Between 2006 and 2015*. Pretoria: Statistics South Africa.
Strand, Håvard, Siri Aas Rustad, Håvard Mokleiv Nygård and Håvard Hegre. (2020). *Trends in Armed Conflict, 1946–2019*. Conflict Trends 8. Oslo: PRIO. Viewed from: https://reliefweb.int/report/world/trends-armed-conflict-1946-2019. [Date accessed: July 5, 2022].
Stout, Jeffrey. (2005). *Democracy and Tradition*. Princeton, NJ: Princeton University Press.
Surkes, Sue. (2019). *Supreme Court Rules for Jewish Group in Battle Over Old City Church Leases*. Times of Israel, 12 June. Viewed from: https://www.timesofisrael.com/supreme-court-rules-for-jewish-group-in-battle-over-old-city-church-leases/. [Date accessed: May 30, 2022].
Swiss Coalition for Corporate Justice. (2020). *Details About the Initiative*. Viewed from: https://corporatejustice.ch/about-the-initiative/. [Date accessed: May 30, 2022].
Tetzlaff, Rainer. (2009). "Armutsminderung in der Dritten Welt: moralische Verpflichtung oder politische Illusion?" in Theodor Hanf, Hans N. Weiler and Helga Dickow (eds.), *Entwicklung als Beruf*. Baden-Baden: Nomos, 473–484.
Thompson, Sarah. (2020). *COVID-19's "Shadow Pandemic" Driving Early Marriage*. Viewed from: https://berkleycenter.georgetown.edu/posts/covid-19-s-shadow-pandemic-driving-early-marriage. [Date accessed: March 4, 2022].
The Cambridge Mosque Trust. (n.d.). *Environment*. Viewed from: https://cambridgecentralmosque.org/environment/. [Date accessed: July 2, 20220].
The Islamic Foundation for Ecology and Environmental Sciences (IFEES). (2015). *Islamic Declaration on Global Climate Change*. Viewed from: https://www.ifees.org.uk/about/islamic-declaration-on-global-climate-change/. [Date accessed: August 28, 2022].
The President and Fellows of Harvard College. (2016). *Religion and Global Health: An Interview with Dr. Susan Holman*. Initiative on Health, Religion, And Spirituality. Viewed from: https://projects.iq.harvard.edu/rshm/religion-and-global-health-interview-dr-susan-holman. [Date accessed: July 31, 2022].
The Shalom Center. (2015). *A Rabbinic Letter on the Climate Crisis*. Viewed from: https://theshalomcenter.org/civicrm/petition/sign?sid=17. [Date accessed: August 28, 2022].
Togarasei, Lovemore. (2011). "The Pentecostal Gospel of Prosperity in African Contexts of Poverty: An Appraisal", *Exchange* 40: 336–350.
Tolstoy, Leo. (2022). *In Search for Meaning of Life*. Viewed from: https://edubirdie.com/examples/leo-tolstoy-in-search-for-meaning-of-life/. [Date accessed: August, 21, 2022].
Tomalin, Emma, Jörg Haustein and Shabaana Kidy. (2019). "Religion and the Sustainable Development Goals", *The Review of Faith & International Affairs*, 17(2): 102–118. 10.1080/15570274.2019.1608664.
Udenrigsministeriet/Ministry of Foreign Affairs of Denmark. (2019). *Unlocking the potential of Interreligious Dialogues for Sustainable Development?* Denmark: Sustainia.
United Nations (UN). (n.d.). *We Can End Poverty. Millennium Development Goals and Beyond 2015*. Viewed from: https://www.un.org/millenniumgoals/poverty.shtml. [Date accessed: August 5, 2022].
United Nations Population Fund (UNFPA). (2014). "Religion and Development Post-2015". Edited by Azza Karam. Report of a Consultation among Donor Organizations,

United Nations Development Agencies and Faith-Based Organizations. Viewed from: https://www.unfpa.org/sites/default/files/pub-pdf/DONOR-UN-FBO%20May%202014.pdf.UNFPA. [Date accessed: May 30, 2022].

United Nations Population Fund (UNFPA). (2016). "Realizing the Faith Dividend: Religion, Gender, Peace and Security in Agenda 2030". Edited by Azza Karam. Technical Report. UNFPA.

United Nations (UN). (1948). *Universal Declaration of Human Rights*. Viewed from: https://www.un.org/en/about-us/universal-declaration-of-human-rights. [Date accessed: August 31, 2022].

United Nations (UN). (2015). *Millennium Development Goal Report*. Viewed from: http://www.un.org/millenniumgoals/. [Date accessed: May 30, 2022].

United Nations Framework Convention on Climate Change (UNFCCC). (2021). World Religious Leaders and Scientists Make pre-CoP26 Appeal. 5 October 2021. https://unfccc.int/news/world-religious-leaders-and-scientists-make-pre-cop26-appeal. [Date accessed: August 28, 2022]

United Nations Climate Change. (2021). *Religious Leaders Issue Joint Appeal Ahead of COP26*. September 8. Viewed from: https://unfccc.int/news/religious-leaders-issue-joint-appeal-ahead-of-cop26. [Date accessed: August 28, 2022].

United Nations. Department of Economic and Social Affairs (UNDESA). (n.d.). *Do You Know All 17 SDGs?* https://sdgs.un.org/goals. [Date accessed: August 15, 2022].

United Nations. Department of Economic and Social Affairs (UNDESA). (2022). *Sustainable Development Goals Report 2021*. Viewed from: https://unstats.un.org/sdgs/report/2021/. [Date accessed: July 9, 2022].

United Nations Development Programme (UNDP). (2020). *Human Development Report 2020*. Viewed from: https://hdr.undp.org/content/human-development-report-2020. [Date accessed: May 30, 2022].

United Nations Development Programme (UNDP). (2022). *Gender Inequality Index*. Viewed from: http://hdr.undp.org/en/content/gender-inequality-index-gii. [Date accessed: March 4, 2022].

United Nations Educational, Scientific and Cultural Organisation (UNESCO). (2021). *Global Education Monitoring Report*. Viewed from: https://en.unesco.org/gem-report/report-education-all-efa. [Date accessed: July 31, 2022].

Van Gennep, Arnold. (2004). *The Rites of Passage*. London: Routledge.

Vaughan, Megan. (1991). *Curing Their Ills: Colonial Power and African Illness*. Stanford, CA: Stanford University Press.

Waardenburg, Jacques. (1986). *Religionen und Religion: Systematische Einführung in die Religionswissenschaft*. Berlin: de Gruyter.

Wahid, Abdurrahman and Daisaku Ikeda. (2015). "Culture Exchange is the Source of Creativity", in Abdurrahman Wahid and Daisaku Ikeda (eds.), *The Wisdom of Tolerance: A Philosophy of Generosity and Peace*. London: I.B. Tauris & Co. Ltd, 64–70.

Ware, Vicki-Ann, Anthony Ware and Matthew Clarke. (2016). "Domains of faith impact: how 'faith' is perceived to shape faith-based international development organisations", *Development in Practice* 26(3): 321–333. 10.1080/09614524.2916.1149150.

Weber, Max. (1994). *Wissenschaft als Beruf*. Tübingen: Mohr Siebeck.

Welker, Michael. (2013). "Global Public Theology and Christology", in Heinrich Bedford-Strohm, Florian Höhne and Tobias Reitmeier (eds.), *Contextuality and Intercontextuality*. Proceedings from the Bamberg Conference, 23–25 June 2011, Münster: Lit, 281–290.

White, Lynn Jr. (1967). "The Historical Roots of our Ecological Crisis", *Science* 155: 1203–1207.

White, Peter. (2020). "Religion, Culture and Development: The Pneuma-Diaconal Perspective of African Pentecostalism", *Stellenbosch Theological Journal* 6(2): 459–478. 10.17570/stj.2020.v6n4.a21.

White, Peter. (2022). "The Future of African Pentecostal Scholarship: The Role of the Church and Academia", in Dave Johnson and Rick Wadholm Jr. (eds.), *Theological Education in the Majority World: Volume 1*. Philippines: APTS Press, 127–144.

White, Peter and Rachel Pauline Aikins. (2021). "Name It, Claim It, Grab It: African Neo-Pentecostal Faith and Hope Gospel", *Journal of Pentecostal Theology* 30(2): 263–281.

Whitehead, C. (2005). "The Historiography of British Imperial Education Policy. Part II: Africa and the Rest of the Colonial Empire", *History of Education* 34: 441–454.

Widmer, Mariana, Ana P. Betran, Mario Merialdi, Jennifer Requejo and Ted Karpf. (2011). "The Role of Faith-Based Organizations in Maternal and Newborn Health Care in Africa", *International Journal of Gynecology & Obstetrics* 114(3): 218–222. 10.1016/j.ijgo.2011.03.015.

Wilkinson, Olivia. (2021). "Putting the 'Strategic' into Strategic Religious Engagement", *The Review of Faith & International Affairs* 19(sup1): 78–84, 10.1080/15570274.2021.1983361.

Wilson, Brian C. (1998). "From the Lexical to the Polythetic: A Brief History of the Definition of Religion", in Thomas A. Idinopulos and Brian C. Wilson (eds.), *What is Religion? Origins, Definitions, and Explanations*. Leiden: Brill, 141–162.

World Bank. (1990). *World Bank Development Report*. Oxford: Oxford University Press.

World Bank. (2014). "Faith Based and Religious Organizations". Viewed from: https://www.worldbank.org/en/about/partners/brief/faith-based-organizations. [Date accessed: September 5, 2022].

World Bank. (2020). Poverty – Overview. October 07. Viewed from: https://www.worldbank.org/en/topic/poverty/overview. [Date accessed: May 30, 2022].

World Commission on Environment and Development (WCED). (1987). *Our common future*. Viewed from: www.un-documents.net/our-common-future.pdf. [Date accessed: September 5, 2022].

World Population Review. (2022). *Religion by Country 2022*. Viewed from: https://worldpopulationreview.com/country-rankings/religion-by-country. [Date accessed: September 7, 2022].

World Vision. (2022). *Child marriage: Facts, FAQs, and how to help end it*. Viewed from: https://www.worldvision.org/child-protection-news-stories/child-marriage-facts. [Date accessed: March 4, 2022].

INDEX

Abrahamic religions 76, 116
accountability 51, 116
actors 1, 3–5, 10, 14, 17, 18, 20, 22, 24, 25, 28, 33, 34, 37, 42, 46, 47, 66, 112–114; Christian 55; development 38, 40, 50, 78, 96, 113, 116; external 50; faith 1, 3–5, 17, 18–27, 29, 32, 33, 35, 37–42, 47, 55, 56, 58–60, 66, 67, 71, 77, 105–107, 115; faith-based 113–116; non-religious 14; political 50; religious 4, 17, 23, 40, 47, 61, 64, 86, 94, 96, 97, 105, 113; secular 3, 33, 39, 42, 107, 113, 114
African Traditional Religion (ATR) 25
Agenda 2030 5, 17, 18, 23
apartheid 51, 52, 88

bilingual/bilinguality 31, 114
Boko Haram 13
Buddhism 11–13, 40, 55, 71, 72, 74, 95, 112

child marriage 75–79
Christian Action for Reconciliation and Social Assistance (CARSA) 39, 109, 110
Christianity 11–13, 19, 27, 28, 46–48, 51, 66, 87, 93, 94, 112, 116
Catholicism 11, 13, 56, 110
church and state 29–31; relationship between 29
churches 1, 4, 13, 14, 29–31, 50–53, 58, 60, 70, 85, 89, 110; African Pentecostal 52, 53; Catholic 59, 76; Charismatic 51; Christian 14, 66, 85, 93, 94, 110; Classical Pentecostal 51; evangelical 77; mainline 22; Mormon 97; Neo-Pentecostal 51; Neo-Prophetic 51; Orthodox 75; Pentecostal 35, 47, 49–53, 111; Protestant 59, 76, 88; *see also* World Council of Churches (WCC)
climate 92–94, 97; action 2, 92, 96, 100; change 10, 15, 17, 31, 45, 92–98, 100, 101; justice 97; *see also* SDGs (SDG 13)
community 26, 29, 34–36, 55, 56, 58, 59, 60, 63, 68, 74, 79, 80, 86, 87, 89, 91, 98–100, 103, 108–111, 113, 115; *see also* religion, as community
conflicts 2, 3, 13–15, 25, 36, 45, 47, 61, 62, 64, 65, 70, 80, 83, 102–107, 109, 113; resolution 13, 69, 70, 82, 103, 104, 107; transformation 21, 33, 103–107
Cooperative Cow Raising 39, 109
COVID-19 45, 47, 54, 58, 60, 61, 63, 65, 75, 77, 84, 92, 112; lockdown/s 45, 47, 61, 65, 75; mitigation measures 62; pandemic 45, 47, 54, 58, 60, 84, 92, 112; prevention 64; prevention training 62, 63
Cows for Peace 109, 110
critics 32; immanent 3, 41, 86, 114, 115

Daoism 13
democracy 62, 65, 69, 88, 91
demographics 11, 13, 25, 26, 110
development 1–5, 7, 9, 11, 12, 15, 17–21, 23–42, 45, 48, 49, 53, 56, 58, 60, 61–68, 70, 78, 79, 86, 88, 89, 102, 107–109, 112–116; global 10, 21, 22, 24, 42, 112; international 12, 19, 23, 27, 33, 113
dynamics 25, 26

education 2, 15, 27, 28, 37, 49, 51, 52, 55, 56, 61, 64–70, 71, 72, 74, 77, 79, 81, 95, 96, 98, 102, 109, 111, 114, 117; for all 65, 66; *see also* health; holistic 69; missionary 19; provider/s 65, 69–71; quality 71; of religious personnel and advocacy 68; system/s 66, 67, 69–71, 77, 89; wisdom and human values in 71; *see also* religion; religious; SDGs (SDG 4)
empire 12, 55, 56, 66, 87, 88
engagements 3, 4, 19, 22, 23, 27, 29, 32, 37, 42, 49, 50, 59, 61, 78, 79, 86, 94, 105, 107, 109, 112, 114, 115; evidence-based faith 18; inter-faith 94; multifaith 116; multi-religious 112; *see also* religious
Enlightenment 9, 93; post- 3, 10, 19, 30
environment 17, 18, 21, 29, 31, 42, 93–96, 98–101, 117
environmental 18, 95; care 94; change 100; concerns 93, 94; crisis 93, 96; exploitation 93; issues 94, 95, 97; management 100, 101; matters 96; problems 94, 96; protection 96; sustainability 93
equal partners 42

faith 2, 3, 18–20, 23, 24, 27, 29–33, 37–39, 42, 51, 52, 57, 58, 62, 63, 71, 72, 77–79, 81–83, 94, 96, 109, 110, 112–116; Christian 30, 31, 66, 110, 111; communities 1, 17, 23, 34, 40, 56, 58, 60, 63, 80, 82, 83, 115, 117; tradition/s 1–5, 14, 19, 20, 26, 31, 32, 38, 41, 55, 60, 62, 76, 86, 94, 95, 97, 107, 112, 114–116; *see also* actors
Faith and Hope Gospel *see* gospel
faith-based 5, 34, 40, 56, 67–71, 74, 98, 104, 107, 110, 113, 114; education providers 67–71; health providers (FBHPs) 55–57, 60; non- 22; organisation/s (FBOs) 4, 13, 23, 37, 115; reconciliation initiatives 109
female genital mutilation (FGM) 61, 75, 76, 79
forgiveness 81, 104, 105, 107–111
formal contributions 41, 42
framework 3, 9, 17, 28, 29, 32, 39, 42, 46, 48, 50, 56, 69, 71, 72, 74, 92, 97, 105–107, 113, 116; *see also* religion as
fundamentalists 89, 90
fundraising 36

gender-based violence (GBV) 64, 79, 112
gender equality 2, 38, 40, 76–80, 83, 102, 117; *see also* SDGs (SDG 5)

gender inequality 78–80, 83
genocidaire 39, 109, 110
genocide 106, 108; post- 14, 39, 107, 108, 110, 111; Rwandan 107; *see also* perpetrators; survivors
global 2, 10–12, 14, 15, 17, 18, 21, 22, 29, 31, 32, 47, 54, 56, 62, 64, 65, 67, 68, 70, 79, 84–86, 92–96, 101–103, 116; development 21–24, 42, 45, 113; diplomacy 15; disruption of health care improvements 54; North 12, 17, 47, 57; South 12, 17, 47, 57
glocal 31
good health and well-being 55; *see also* SDGs (SDG 3)
gospel 30, 48, 50, 51, 53, 88; Prosperity 47–50; Faith and Hope 51

healing 14, 62, 104, 106, 108–111 *see* holistic
health 1, 18, 28, 37, 47, 48, 51, 52, 54–57, 59, 60–64, 77, 79, 116; and education 17, 55, 61; and well-being 56–58, 98; care 1, 31, 54–58, 60, 61; good 55; needs; policies 55; public 60, 61–63; security 62; services 54, 55, 61; systems 55, 58, 61; *see also* religion; SDGs (SDG 3)
Hinduism 11, 71
holistic 4, 13, 19, 21, 39, 52, 69, 70, 74, 88, 96, 97, 101, 106, 107; development 39, 41, 109; healing 54, 57
human dignity 80, 85, 89, 114
human rights 14, 29, 31, 41, 42, 62, 79, 84–89, 91, 103, 104, 114, 115; *see also* religion
hunger 2, 15, 28, 45, 97, 102; zero 5; *see also* SDGs (SDG 2)
Hutu 107, 108

identity/identities 4, 20, 26, 34, 35, 41, 69, 80, 83, 108
impact 2, 5, 14, 15, 19, 42, 47, 48, 57, 58, 60, 63, 68, 71, 76, 77, 97, 102, 104, 112, 116; measuring 116
inclusion 21–24, 26, 40, 57, 67, 68, 71, 86, 87, 107
incompatibility with SDGs 39, 40
inequality 41, 53, 71, 78–80, 83–85, 87
institution/s 3, 14, 15, 24, 26, 28, 29, 36, 46, 47, 59, 61, 62, 64, 66–68, 70, 79, 87, 95, 97, 103, 106, 113; religion 1, 28, 36, 60, 70, 79, 106; *see also* religion; SDGs (SDG 16)

international non-governmental organisation (INGO) 19, 20
Islam 11–13, 25, 37, 40, 46, 71, 72, 79, 80, 81, 83, 94, 95, 106, 116
Israel 14, 62, 88–90, 91

Jews 11, 26, 63, 76, 89–91, 105
Judaism 11, 12, 40, 76, 88, 91, 116

kingdom, secular 30; spiritual 30; doctrine of the two 29

#LaudatoSiLent 96
leadership 13, 28, 51, 75–77, 81; religious 68, 115
Lent 96
love 1, 3, 22, 26, 27, 30, 48, 53, 85, 87, 90, 91, 105

madrasas 68, 70, 77, 78
material contributions 41
meaning 27, 34, 38, 39, 46, 47, 57, 74, 87, 99, 106
Millennium Development Goals (MDGs) 17, 18, 22, 45
missio Dei 53
missionaries 18, 19, 48, 56, 57, 66, 67
mosques 1, 4, 14, 89
Muhammad, Prophet 80, 81
multilingual 114
multi-religious 26, 60, 62, 63, 112, 117; advocacy 62; movement 62; narratives 116; perspectives 60; services 62; solidarity 62; value added 64

non-governmental organisation (NGO) 19–22, 24, 33, 37, 39, 40, 47, 61, 77, 88, 109
norms 26, 37, 41, 78, 83, 95, 96

paradigm 5, 19, 21, 29, 30, 35; shift/s 22, 38, 73, 95, 97
peace 1, 2, 10, 13–15, 21, 27, 36, 40, 62, 63, 70, 79, 86, 88, 94, 102–109, 111–113, 115–117; *see also* Cows for Peace; Religions for Peace
peace and justice 18, 102; *see also* SDGs (SDG 16)
peacebuilding 103–107, 116; interreligious 116; religious 104, 116
peacemaking 104; efforts 14, 104
Pentecostal/s 48, 49, 51–53, 63, 112; African 51; *see also* churches; poverty alleviation; theology

Pentecostalism 47, 48, 50–53; classical 51, 53
perpetrators 39, 103, 106–109, 111
perspectives 3, 5, 9, 10, 19, 25, 31, 32, 34, 38, 41, 64, 66, 67, 74, 78, 79, 80, 83, 94, 95, 98, 100, 104, 106, 114, 116; anthropocentric 93; Buddhist 71, 72, 74; Christian 51, 107; of Christian public theology 29, 31; demonic influence 51; eschatological 106; faith-based 110; global 31; holistic 52, 88; indigenous 3, 98; Jewish 88; multi-religious 60; Muslim 80, 94; philosophical 72; theological 56, 93
pluralism 69, 71
pneuma-diaconal, approach 52; ministry 53
policymakers 3–5, 14, 15, 18, 104, 112–114
potentials 26, 33, 34, 39, 42, 50, 60, 70, 107, 113
poverty 2, 15, 17, 19, 49–52, 63, 65, 70, 77, 89, 93, 110; alleviation 19, 22–24, 45–52, 102, 112; countering 51; line 45, 51; political factors 51; social interpretation of 49; structural factors 51; theological interpretation of 49; transformation of 49; *see also* SDGs
practice 18, 19, 23, 24, 26, 29, 36, 37, 41, 46, 49, 50, 52, 57, 59, 68, 71, 73, 75, 78, 79, 83, 87, 97, 99, 100, 112, 113, 115, 116; *see also* religion
practitioners 3–5, 14, 18, 25, 40, 83, 104, 112–114, 116
proselytisation 39, 40, 107
Protestantism 13

reconciliation 27, 39, 103–113; cell groups 109
relationship/s 20, 21, 26, 27, 29, 34, 39, 46, 47, 49, 59, 62, 66, 70, 72, 82, 86, 87, 95, 101, 102, 104, 105, 107, 109; building 26, 35, 37, 105, 107
religion 1–5, 9–15, 18, 19, 23–31, 33–37, 39, 40–42, 46–58, 61–63, 66–69, 71, 72, 74, 76–79, 82, 83, 85–89, 91, 93–96, 103–107, 111–114, 116, 117; as community 3, 26, 34, 35, 39, 40, 59, 68, 86, 105; and/in development 3, 7, 21, 22, 25, 39; faces of/different faces 3, 25, 113; as framework 3, 28, 38, 46, 49, 71, 88, 97, 106; green 92; health 57, 60; history of 93; and human rights 85; as institution/s 3, 28, 36, 47, 60, 70, 79, 87, 106; instrumentalising 82; matters 1, 2, 9, 13, 16, 55, 66–68, 75, 84, 102, 112; as

networks 41; and poverty 46, 47; as practice 3, 27, 34–39, 41, 46, 47, 49, 59, 78, 87, 96, 113; in public 14, 89; rediscovering 9, 10, 18; as religio-scape 3, 25; and the SDGs 1, 2, 3, 4, 17, 43; spirituality 3, 27, 34–36, 38, 40, 41, 46, 69, 96, 106; as teachings 3, 26, 37, 38, 40, 41, 46–48, 56, 59, 68, 78, 95, 105, 113; violent conflict 103

religio-scape *see* religion

Religions for Peace (RfP) 14, 60, 62–64, 117

religious 2, 4, 9–15, 18–20, 23, 26–28, 34–37, 39–42, 46, 47, 49, 55–62, 64, 66–71, 73–83, 85–91, 95–97, 104–107, 110–117; cleaning 26; communities 4, 15, 23, 35, 36, 39, 40, 61; education 69; engagements 15, 113; illiteracy 15, 80; leaders 4, 34, 58–64, 68, 78, 79, 93–95, 106, 115; literacy 15, 16, 28, 68, 69, 114; minorities 26, 42, 86; non-governmental organisations (RNGOs) 19, 20; practices 28; -secular divide 4, 112; *see also* actors; rituals

resilience 38, 47, 61, 82

rights 10, 14, 29, 38, 39, 62, 76, 77, 79, 80–83, 85, 86–91; minority 86, 88, 89; *see also* human rights

rituals 27, 28, 33, 59, 60, 61, 78, 79, 106

service delivery 28, 33, 34, 37, 39, 40, 60, 70, 106

social media 115, 116

solidarity 1, 13, 22, 27, 28, 56, 62, 69, 72, 88, 109, 112, 115

spheres 2, 4, 10, 13, 30, 114; private 30, 79; public 9, 12, 15, 19, 79; public-secular 30; religious 12, 36, 39, 55, 57, 58, 69; religious-private 30

spirituality 3, 11, 27, 29, 31, 34, 96, 98, 99, 113; eco- 95, 96; *see also* religion as spirituality

strategic religious engagement (SRE) 23, 113

Sub-Saharan Africa 19, 45, 54, 66, 103

survivors 82, 106–109, 111

Sustainable Development Goals (SDGs) 1–4, 15, 17, 18, 23, 24, 29, 33, 38–41, 43, 92, 102, 112–116; SDG 1 "No Poverty" 2, 5, 45; SDG 2 "Zero Hunger" 2, 5, 45; SDG 3 "Good Health and Well-Being" 5, 54, 60; SDG 4 "Quality Education" 5, 65, 67; SDG 5 "Gender Equality" 2, 5, 40, 75, 76, 79, 115; SDG 10 "Reduced Inequalities" 5, 84, 85; SDG 13 "Climate Action" 2, 3, 5, 92; SDG 16 "Peace, Justice and Strong Institutions" 5, 40, 102; SDG 17 40; *see also* religion

state 13, 21, 30, 31, 47, 69, 70, 71, 77, 86, 88–91, 102; *see also* church and state

symbols 27

synagogues 14

teachings 20, 26–29, 40, 41, 47, 49, 70, 71, 78, 79, 80, 83, 87, 90, 91, 95–100, 105, 113; *see also* religion

theology 29, 30, 32, 68, 72, 74, 85, 114; academic; biblical 51; Christian 29, 30, 85, 115; eco- 96; liberation 51; matters; Pentecostal 49; public 29–32; psycho- 51

traditional ecological knowledge 3, 98, 100

transformation 21, 33, 35, 36, 38, 40, 41, 48, 46, 49, 51, 70, 72, 74, 80, 97, 103–107; personal 35, 39, 48, 69

trauma 61, 104, 106, 107, 109, 110

trust 15, 21, 34, 35, 41, 52, 57, 59, 82, 104, 105, 107, 113, 114, 116; generate/generating 34, 35

violence 2, 15, 19, 27, 39, 40, 62, 64, 75, 82, 83, 91, 102–106, 110, 112; against women and girls (VAWG) 76, 79, 80, 82, 83; cultural; direct; domestic 62, 75, 82; non- 40, 87; sexual 82; spiritual 82, 83; structural 103; *see also* gender-based violence (GBV)

women 11, 26, 28, 45, 49, 53, 54, 56, 62–65, 67, 75–86, 100, 107, 115; in focus 115; leaders 81; Muslim 14, 83, 89; voice of 76

World Council of Churches (WCC) 22, 60, 87, 94

World Health Organisation (WHO) 56, 58

youth 34, 51, 63, 70, 87, 89, 92, 107, 109, 115, 116

For Product Safety Concerns and Information please contact our EU representative GPSR@taylorandfrancis.com
Taylor & Francis Verlag GmbH, Kaufingerstraße 24, 80331 München, Germany

www.ingramcontent.com/pod-product-compliance
Lightning Source LLC
Chambersburg PA
CBHW071822230426
43670CB00013B/2536